1732

THE CONCESSIVE RELATION

IN OLD ENGLISH POETRY

BY RANDOLPH QUIRK

ARCHON BOOKS
1973

Library of Congress Cataloging in Publication Data
Quirk, Randolph.
 The concessive relation in Old English poetry.

 Reprint of the ed. published by Yale University Press, New Haven, Conn., which was issued as no. 124 of Yale studies in English; with new pref.
 Bibliography: p.
 1. Anglo-Saxon language—Mood. 2. Anglo-Saxon poetry—History and criticism. I. Title.
II. Series: Yale studies in English, no. 124.
PE225.Q5   1973   429'.82   73–12230
ISBN 0–208–01397–0

[Yale Studies in English, vol. 124]

© 1954 by Yale University Press.

Reprinted 1973 with permission and
with corrections in an unabridged edition
and with a new preface
as an Archon Book, an imprint of
THE SHOE STRING PRESS, INC.
Hamden, Connecticut 06514

Printed in the United States of America

PREFACE

THIS STUDY is intended to be a companion volume to earlier monographs in the Yale Studies in English which investigated the expression of notional relationships, and in particular to Josephine M. Burnham's *Concessive Constructions in Old English Prose*. Like these it is therefore based on the assumption (in practice almost universal) that the meaning of a recorded utterance can be sufficiently determined for research of this kind to provide fit material for linguistic analysis.

Written with the knowledge and, I am grateful to say, encouragement of Professor Burnham, the monograph not only presents an analysis of those literary monuments which were outside the scope of her study but seeks to compare the results thus obtained for Old English poetry with those that she obtained for the prose. Since, however, my approach inevitably differs in some respects from that of Miss Burnham, I have analyzed for myself extensive passages of Old English prose in order to obtain data more strictly commensurable with those which I had assembled for the poetry. In addition, I have naturally taken account of the methods and results of syntactical studies (particularly in the Old English field) published since the appearance of Miss Burnham's volume in 1911.

My work on the Old English expression of the concessive relation began as a piece of research, completed in 1951, for the degree of Doctor of Philosophy in the University of London. Subsequently, with the opportunity afforded by a Commonwealth Fund Fellowship, I was able to continue my study in this field at Yale University, to develop certain lines of thought, and finally to present my results in such a way as to make them complementary to Miss Burnham's.

My primary debt is to the Quain Professor of English in the University of London, Professor A. H. Smith, for his supervision of my research, and for the training, guidance, and friendly help that I have long received from him. But it is a pleasure to record my gratitude also to Professor Norman Davis, University of Glasgow, for the many hours he has devoted to detailed criticism; to Professor Helge Kökeritz, Yale University, for many useful suggestions during the later stages of my work and for his criticisms when reading the manuscript; to Professor Francis P. Magoun, Jr., Harvard University, for his help and encouragement; to Professor Benjamin C. Nangle, editor of Yale Studies in English, for cheerfully dealing with the many problems associated with a difficult manuscript, and for accommodating troublesome trans-Atlantic alterations; to Professor Frederick W. Hilles (chairman), Professor Cleanth Brooks, and other members of the English Faculty of Yale University, for their advice and hospitality; to Mr. James T. Babb and his staff in the Sterling Memorial Library for their great helpfulness and courtesy; to my wife for her patient cooperation in typing, checking, and proofreading; to the committee of the Yale Studies in English for their generous subvention of the publication costs; and finally to the Commonwealth Fund (to whose directors I owe a special debt for their personal interest and encouragement) for the liberality which made possible my stay at Yale and the production of this monograph.

RANDOLPH QUIRK

University College London
March, 1954

PREFACE TO THE 1973 ISSUE

IT IS A pleasure to have the opportunity to remove a good many of the minor errors which appeared in the original printing and at the same time to thank those kindly reviewers (especially R. W. Zandvoort and K. R. Brooks) whose scholarly watchful eyes greatly facilitated that task. More extensive revision, so as—for example—to take account of the contributions made to Old English syntax and general syntactic theory over the past twenty years, would have meant total rewriting, with no guarantee of a significantly better end-product. In any case, the functionally oriented approach originally adopted is more in tune with current theories than it was with those of the early fifties.

RANDOLPH QUIRK

April 1973

Contents

Preface ... iii

Abbreviations ... vii

I. Introduction ... 1
   1. Principles and methods ... 1
   2. The concessive relation ... 4
   3. Previous work on Old English concession ... 10

II. Concessions Formed with *þeah* ... 14
   1. General ... 14
   2. Reinforcement and correlation ... 14
   3. Word order in nondependent members ... 19
   4. The subordinating conjunction ... 21
   5. Word order in dependent members ... 23
   6. The place of dependent *þeah*-members in the sentence ... 26
   7. Mood in concessive sentences containing *þeah* ... 28
   8. Pattern in concessive sentences ... 34
   9. Parallel dependent members ... 35
   10. Concessive phrases with *þeah* ... 36
   11. Elliptical concessions ... 36
   12. *þeah* as 'even though' ... 37
   13. Conditional and other nonconcessive uses of *þeah* ... 38
   14. Inquiry into the relation between various factors ... 39
   15. Latin originals and parallel versions ... 41

III. Nondependent Concessions without *þeah* ... 44
   1. *hwæðere* ... 44
   2. *ac* ... 48
   3. *and* ... 54
   4. *forðon* ... 58
   5. *mid þy* ... 61
   6. *butan* ... 62
   7. *gyt(a), gen(a)* ... 63
   8. *nu* ... 67
   9. *þa* ... 68
   10. *þonne* ... 69
   11. Minor relating elements ... 70
   12. Zero relating element ... 72

IV. Dependent Concessions without *þeah* — 83

1. General — 83
2. Alternative concessions — 83
3. Zero subordinator — 87
4. Concessive *gif* — 88
5. Indefinite concessions — 91
6. Indefinite concessions of degree — 94
7. Indefinite relative concessions: 'whoever' — 98
8. Indefinite relative concessions: 'whatever' — 99
9. Indefinite concessions of place — 101
10. Concessive-equivalent constructions — 102
11. Concessive-equivalent relative members — 103
12. Concessive-equivalent clauses of manner (*swa*-members) — 108
13. Concessive-equivalent temporal members — 112
14. Concessive-equivalent local members — 114
15. Concessive-equivalent causal members — 115
16. Concessive-equivalent substantive members — 116
17. Concessive-equivalent degree members — 117
18. Concessive and concessive-equivalent words and phrases — 119
19. Concessive-equivalent elements without 'even' significance — 120
20. Concessive-equivalent elements with 'even' significance — 123
21. The concessive use of *wiht* — 126
22. *for* — 132
23. 'all' — 132

V. Conclusion — 134

Selected Bibliography — 141

1. Texts — 141
2. General — 142

Index — 147

ABBREVIATIONS

ALISON'S ISLAND: Harold Brighouse, *Alison's Island*, ed. J. W. Marriott (see Bibliography 1, s.n.).

AND: *Andreas*, ASPR II.

ANGLIA: *Anglia Zeitschrift für englische Philologie*, Halle.

ARCHIV: *Archiv für das Studium der neueren Sprachen und Literaturen*, Elberfeld.

ARCHLING: *Archivum Linguisticum*, Glasgow.

ASC: *Anglo-Saxon Chronicle*, ed. C. Plummer (see Bibliography 1, s.n.).

ASPR I-VI: *The Anglo-Saxon Poetic Records*, ed. G. P. Krapp, E. V. K. Dobbie (see Bibliography 1, s.nn.).

AZ: *Azarias*, ASPR III.

BEO: *Beowulf*, ed. F. Klaeber (see Bibliography 1, s.n.).

BO: *Metres* of Boethius; poetical version: ASPR V; prose version: ed. W. J. Sedgefield (see Bibliography 1, s.n.).

BOROUGHS: *The Capture of the Five Boroughs* (ASC Poem), ASPR VI.

BRUN: *The Battle of Brunanburh* (ASC Poem), ASPR VI.

BT, BTS: Bosworth's *Anglo-Saxon Dictionary*, ed. and suppl. T. N. Toller (see Bibliography 2, s.n. J. Bosworth).

CHARM: *The Metrical Charms*, ASPR VI.

CHR: *Christ*, ASPR III.

CHRSAT: *Christ and Satan*, ASPR I.

CORONEDGAR: *The Coronation of Edgar* (ASC Poem), ASPR VI.

DAN: *Daniel*, ASPR I.

DEATHALFRED: *The Death of Alfred* (ASC Poem), ASPR VI.

DEATHEDGAR: *The Death of Edgar* (ASC Poem), ASPR VI.

DEATHEDWARD: *The Death of Edward* (ASC Poem), ASPR VI.

DEOR: *Deor*, ASPR III.

EETS.OS: *The Early English Text Society* (Original Series), London.

EL: *Elene*, ASPR II.

EngSts: *English Studies*, Amsterdam.

EpMS 41: *The Metrical Epilogue to MS 41*, Corpus Christi College, ASPR vi.

EpPastoral: *The Metrical Epilogue to the Pastoral Care*, ASPR vi.

ESt: *Englische Studien*, Leipzig.

Ex: *Exodus*, ASPR i.

Exhort: *An Exhortation to Christian Living*, ASPR vi.

Fasting: *The Seasons for Fasting*, ASPR vi.

Fates: *The Fates of the Apostles*, ASPR ii.

Finn: *The Battle of Finnsburh*, ASPR vi.

Fort: *The Fortunes of Men*, ASPR iii.

FragPs: *Fragments of Psalms*, Benedictine Office, ASPR vi.

Gen: *Genesis*, ASPR i.

Gift: *The Gifts of Men*, ASPR iii.

Gl: *Guthlac*, ASPR iii.

Hell: *The Descent into Hell*, ASPR iii.

HomFrag i: *Homiletic Fragment* i, ASPR ii.

HomFrag ii: *Homiletic Fragment* ii, ASPR iii.

Husband: *The Husband's Message*, ASPR iii.

J(E)GPh: *Journal of (English and) Germanic Philology*, Bloomington, later Urbana.

Jenny: Charles Thomas, *Jenny in the Orchard*, ed. J. W. Marriott (see Bibliography i, s.n.).

Jud: *Judith*, ed. A. S. Cook (see Bibliography i, s.n.).

Jud i: *The Judgment Day* i, ASPR iii.

Jud ii: *The Judgment Day* ii, ASPR vi.

Jul: *Juliana*, ASPR iii.

Leiden: *The Leiden Riddle*, ASPR vi.

Lingua: *Lingua*, Haarlem.

Lord's Prayer ii: *The Lord's Prayer* ii, ASPR vi.

Maldon: *The Battle of Maldon*, ASPR vi.

Max i: *Maxims* i, ASPR iii.

Max ii: *Maxims* ii, ASPR vi.

ABBREVIATIONS

MENOL: *The Menologium*, ASPR vi.

MLN: *Modern Language Notes*, Baltimore.

MLR: *Modern Language Review*, Cambridge.

MPH: *Modern Philology*, Chicago.

NED: *A New English Dictionary* (see Bibliography 2, s.n. J. Murray).

NEOPHIL: *Neophilologus*, Groningen.

ORDER: *The Order of the World*, ASPR iii.

OROS: *King Alfred's Orosius*, ed. H. Sweet (see Bibliography 1, s.n.).

PANTHER: *The Panther*, ASPR iii.

PARPS: *The Paris Psalter*, ASPR v.

PARTRIDGE: *The Partridge*, ASPR iii.

PBBEIT: *Beiträge zur Geschichte der deutschen Sprache und Literatur*, Halle.

PH: *The Phoenix*, ASPR iii.

PHARAOH: *Pharaoh*, ASPR iii.

PHILSOC: *Transactions of the Philological Society*, London.

PMLA: *Publications of the Modern Language Association of America*, Baltimore.

PRAYER: *A Prayer*, ASPR vi.

PREC: *Precepts*, ASPR iii.

PREFDIALOGUES: *The Metrical Preface to Gregory's Dialogues*, ASPR vi.

PSALM 50: *Psalm 50*, ASPR vi.

RESIG: *Resignation*, ASPR iii.

RID: *Riddles*, ASPR iii.

RIMP: *The Riming Poem*, ASPR iii.

ROOD: *The Dream of the Rood*, ASPR ii.

RUIN: *The Ruin*, ASPR iii.

RUNE: *The Rune Poem*, ASPR vi.

RUTHWELL: *The Ruthwell Cross*, ASPR vi.

SEAF: *The Seafarer*, ASPR iii.

SOL: *Solomon and Saturn*, ASPR vi.

SOUL I: *Soul and Body* i, ASPR ii.

SOUL II: *Soul and Body* ii, ASPR iii.

SPE: *Society for Pure English Tracts*, Oxford.

STCLPHIL: *Cornell Studies in Classical Philology*, Ithaca.

STNEOPHIL: *Studia Neophilologica*, Uppsala.

STUDENGPHIL: Morsbach's *Studien zur englischen Philologie*, Halle.

VAIN: *Vainglory*, ASPR III.

VESPPS: *Vespasian Psalter*, in *The Oldest English Texts*, ed. H. Sweet (EETS.OS 83), London 1885.

WALD: *Waldere*, ASPR VI.

WAND: *The Wanderer*, ASPR III.

WHALE: *The Whale*, ASPR III.

WID: *Widsith*, ASPR III.

WIFE: *The Wife's Lament*, ASPR III.

WULF: *Wulf and Eadwacer*, ASPR III.

Other abbreviations used are those generally current in linguistic and literary studies.

I

Introduction

1. PRINCIPLES AND METHODS

SYNTAX may be studied "from two points of view. We can either start from the grammatical forms, and explain their uses . . . or we may take a grammatical category, and describe the different forms by which it is expressed . . ."[1] As G. W. Small points out, almost all the studies in English syntax up to now have adopted the former of Sweet's two methods, although there are outstanding exceptions in the space given to relationship in the works of Sweet himself, Poutsma, Jespersen, and Curme. We must concentrate, says Small, on relationship and function, in a combination of the descriptive, historical, and comparative approaches. There is now, he adds, no room for the pure descriptivism of 1910.[2]

In point of fact there is no English grammar written along these lines. France has been more fortunate; there is the vast and somewhat subjective *La Pensée et la langue* in which Brunot resolutely starts from the notional point of view and explores the whole of the French resources, Part v dealing entirely with the subject of grammatical relations and the means of expressing them. There is also Eugen Lerch's *Historische französische Syntax* which, rejecting the 19th-century equation of *syntax* with *Satzlehre*, treats syntax as the investigation of how the mental categories (such as *desire, command,* and the like) are expressed in language. This book begins by exploring all the possible approaches to syntactical study (descriptive, logical, comparative, genetic, psychological, aesthetic, historical), and its significance extends far beyond the limits of French grammar.

In the present study, instead of starting with *form* and working to *function,* we start with *function* and work to *form.* That is to say, it is not a case of taking an individual word, as Maisenhelder takes OE *and,* and then examining all the functions that it performs, but rather of taking a notional relationship, investigating all its occurrences,

---

1. Sweet, *New English Grammar* 1.§582.
2. PMLA li.1–7; cf. Bosker's admirable survey of the formal and functional criteria in syntax, Neophil xxxi.28f.

and then classifying all the grammatical forms in which the relationship is expressed.

The methods involved can be stated briefly. We begin by analyzing the *whole context* in order to arrive at the total meaning. This is then tested by translation and paraphrase in as great a variety of ways as possible. We may then see what is substitutable for the construction under review in another language or stratum of the same language. Thirdly, any variant manuscript readings have to be studied, because although we may be dealing simply with a scribal misinterpretation we may well find what to the scribe appeared alternative and synonymous forms for expressing the relationship. Fourthly, where the text has an extant source, be it in the same language or another, this must be studied, not merely to have a check on the interpretation, but to note again alternative forms of expression or to observe the influence of one language or literary style upon another.[3]

In connection with the fourth point, we must beware of relying too much on a Latin original for our interpretation of the OE text before us. Quite apart from the well-known fact that OE translators felt by no means obliged always to follow their original closely, we shall see that there are many cases in which the translator misunderstands his original completely. When he does so, this does not necessarily invalidate the form of the construction he uses of course, however mistaken it is from the point of view of translating. Moreover, there are times when a translator may put the emphasis differently and so change the nature of the relationship. Finally, as Ælfric himself tells us in connection with his own translations from the Latin, "ðæt Leden 7 ðæt Englisc nabbað na ane wisan on ðære spræce fandunge." [4]

It is important at the outset to have no preconceived ideas about what data will be useful. It is not enough to collect, for example, a line-reference to *þeah* together with the mood of the verb and perhaps one or two other fragmentary details. At this stage one cannot know what is significant and what is not, and so the whole context of every sentence in which a concessive relation exists (or is suspected to exist) must be accurately copied and filed, regardless of the fact that the cumbersome collection of material must contain not only irrelevant features but perhaps many nonconcessive examples. Only when we have the material as a whole can we start rejecting and classifying examples and singling out significant features, having done everything possible to ensure that the description and analysis are objective.

Even so, one can hardly be equipped to survey the field of concessive

---

3. Cf. Behre's review of Ohlander's *Coordinate Expressions*, EngSts xx.141.
4. Preface to *Genesis* in *The Old English Heptateuch* (ed. S. J. Crawford, EETS.OS 160 [London 1921]) 79.

expression in a past form of English without knowing the range of expression in modern English as well. The current grammars of English are an inadequate guide since they tend to concentrate not only on the formal aspects of concession but solely on the formal aspects in the literary language; the average grammar merely tells us that concession is expressed with (*al*)*though* and sometimes adds notes on correlative or coordinate constructions with *yet* and *nevertheless*. It is better to carry out a limited survey of current English on the same lines as the survey of the OE literature. For this reason, the range of concessive expression has been studied in a few contemporary plays, selected by virtue of being written since the second World War entirely in educated colloquial English, without the intrusion of foreign or dialect-speaking characters. The kind of constructions found and the proportions in which they occurred have been of the utmost interest for purposes of comparison in handling the facts of OE concession, and most of the illustrations from modern English given below in the discussion of OE constructions are from these plays. It was particularly helpful in dealing with the nondependent OE constructions (especially those using *ac* and *and*) to know that in modern English speech, as opposed to the literary language, the usual concessive construction is the nondependent one with *but*. Thus simple *but*-concessions occur by the score in dramatic dialogue to every instance of a dependent *though*-concession, while in stage directions quite a different style is found: ' He is fifteen, and, though he wears only flannel trousers and an open-neck shirt, there is something about his appearance which . . .' (Jenny).

A word is necessary on the conventions adopted for reference and quotation, and also on the grammatical terminology. Reference to the material is by the abbreviated title of the text (on which see the table of abbreviations, pp. xi-xiv) and a number which is usually the line number in the edition used. The exceptions are few; in the case of the *Paris Psalter* there are two numbers given with each reference, the first being the number of the psalm, the second the number of the verse; with certain other texts too there are two numbers, notably the *Riddles* and the Boethian *Metres*, but in these the second number is the line reference, the first being the number of the poem in the edition used. Prose texts are cited by reference to page and line of a particular edition, except that for quotations from the *Anglo-Saxon Chronicle* references are to the manuscript (Plummer's code) and the annal.

It should be noted that references are not usually to the line or verse in which a particular connective or other form is to be found, but rather to the line or verse where we find the beginning of the *whole concessive sequence* in which it occurs.

All quotations follow the text, spelling, punctuation, and arrangement of the edition used, the editor's departures from the manuscript reading being recorded in a footnote. Since, however, the bulk of the material consists of quotations from *The Anglo-Saxon Poetic Records* (ASPR), the conventions of this edition are followed for other material too, accents and such editorial diacritics as length marks being omitted.

The grammatical terminology, in which there have been as few departures as possible from traditional usage, needs little comment. The terms *coordinate* and *paratactic* are unsatisfactory because they are ambiguous, some grammarians using them as synonymous, others as mutually exclusive terms, whereas *nondependent* (naturally opposed to *dependent* in place of *subordinate*) can describe all forms of relationship not involving grammatical subordination, whether there is a relating element (conjunction or adverb) or whether there is none; by this token, *zero relating element* describes the latter form more clearly—if less euphoniously—than *parataxis* does. Finally, *member* is convenient, since unlike *clause* it can embrace 'although he was rude' and 'for all his rudeness.'

2. THE CONCESSIVE RELATION

To many grammarians the concessive relation is a special form of the adversative relation. By this they mean that when two parts of an utterance are made to oppose or to contrast with one another, that is, are related *adversatively*, they may at the same time be related *concessively*, depending on the nature or degree of the contrast; all concessive relations are adversative, but not all adversative relations are concessive. This is implicit, for example, in the classification of concession by Western and Zandvoort [5] and is given full expression again and again by Lerch in his detailed analysis of concession. To him, the adversative relation becomes concessive when the opposition is so great that the content of the dependent member normally excludes the content of the nondependent one.[6]

But analyzing the difference between the concessive and adversative relations, a problem which will engage us below in presenting the OE *ac* material (III.2), is not the same as defining either of them. Some scholars have seen the essence of concession in Wilmanns' idea of

---

5. *De Engelske Bisætninger* 41f., and *A Handbook of English Grammar* (Groningen 1950) §641 respectively.
6. *Historische französische Syntax* 1.195. Cf. 1.199, 263.

the 'Herausforderung' function of the subjunctive;[7] thus Schücking, after commenting on the inadequacy of previous definitions of concession, draws attention to the 'challenge' formula which not only says that one part of the relation is irrelevant to the other, but (he contends) makes an actual challenge that the other part is valid despite it.[8]

In his study of the subjunctive and optative in Sanskrit and Greek, Delbrück had insisted on the basic connection between the reluctant wish and concession,[9] and Onions maintains it in *An Advanced English Syntax* (see §38), which first appeared in 1903. But, says Glunz, in the sentence *sint sane Rhodienses superbi, quid id ad nos attinet?* it is not true that *sint* expresses a reluctant wish; on the contrary it is commanding and defiant, even to the point of having general application; the subjunctive can even be replaced by an imperative, readily recognizable as challenging in character. The subjunctive thus expresses not a wish but a challenge, which in the whole sentence context forms a concession.[1]

As a corollary to this, Glunz himself (op.cit.53) suggests a simplified definition which is not far from Burnham's point of view when she says, "The simple concession contains a fact or notion *in spite of* which the main proposition stands."[2] Similarly Curme: "The concessive clause contains a conceded statement, which, though it is naturally in contrast or opposition to that of the principal proposition, is nevertheless unable to destroy the validity of the latter" (*Syntax* 332). More recently we have, among others, Dr. Charleston's definition on the same lines: "A clause is concessive when it embodies a predication, seemingly at variance or in conflict or incompatible with the sense of the main clause, which is accepted as not vitiating the truth of the main clause."[3]

With only a slight shift of emphasis, the conflict and opposition can be regarded as constituting an inoperative or inadequate obstacle. This is the line adopted by Erdmann to which Schücking (op.cit.§15) takes exception, and it forms the background to Kuhlmann's statement that "Konzessivsätze sind alle diejenigen Sätze, in denen etwas zugegeben wird, was—obwohl es an sich dazu geeignet wäre—die Gültigkeit

---

7. *Deutsche Grammatik* III.I.261.
8. *Die Grundzüge der Satzverknüpfung* §15a.
9. *Syntaktische Forschungen* (B. Delbrück, E. Windisch, Halle 1871) I.27: "Der Wunsch ist nicht aus der freien Initiative des Wünschenden hervorgegangen, sondern ist ihm abgerungen."
1. *Die Verwendung des Konjunktivs* 53.
2. *Concessive Constructions in Old English Prose* 4 (her italics); in future, the frequent references to this study will be by the author's name and the page numbers only.
3. *Studies on the Syntax of the English Verb* 145.

des Hauptsatzes dennoch im gegebenen Falle nicht aufhebt."[4] "A concessive clause," says Behre, " serves to introduce an obstacle which is not sufficient to prevent the realisation of the idea expressed in the main clause."[5] Similarly, Urban Ohlander uses this criterion to distinguish causal and concessive functions of *and* in Middle English; when the first part is " an obstacle (though insufficient) to the realisation of the second," the " relational aspect " is concessive.[6]

A simpler and at the same time a more widely valid definition is obtained when one concentrates on the unexpectedness involved in concession. " Konzessiv nennt man Satzgefüge, in denen ausgedrückt werden soll, dass der Inhalt des Nebensatzes, obwohl man es an und für sich erwarten sollte, für die Aussage des Hauptsatzes nicht in Betracht kommt."[7] Similarly Behaghel characterizes concession as the relationship existing when one member has validity contrary to expectation raised in the other.[8] Poutsma significantly calls concession the ' arrestive adversative ' relation, which obtains when one member states the opposite of the conclusion expected from the other.[9] Jespersen also starts from the adversative relation, ' contrast,' and says that in passing over to concession, which he calls ' contradiction,' " an element of unexpectedness in the factual co-existence then enters into the collocation."[1]

All the approaches which we have passed in review have their own validity, but it would seem that only a very involved or, paradoxically, a very simple definition would cover all the facets of the concessive relation. Perhaps the most satisfactory statement to use as a working guide is simply that *the concessive relation may be said to exist between two parts of an utterance when one part is surprising in view of the other.*

That there is notional connection between concession and other relationships is obvious from the most cursory glance at the relational functions of such elements as *cum, quand même, si, while, but, if.* In both condition and concession, as Burnham says, " the main proposition is thought of as *conditioned* by the subordinate," the concessive sentence containing a hypothesis and a conclusion independent of it (pp. 1–2). Kuhlmann too points out the nearness of concession to condition (*Die Konzessivsätze* 8) and Sweet says, " *Concessive* clauses

---

4. *Die Konzessivsätze im Nibelungenliede* 8. Cf. also Mensing, *Untersuchungen über die Syntax der Concessivsätze* 5.
5. *Subjunctive in Old English Poetry* 118.
6. *Studies in Coordinate Expressions* 17.
7. Wilmanns, *Deutsche Grammatik* III.I.260.
8. *Deutsche Syntax* III.§1421.
9. *Grammar of Late Modern English* I.II.590.
1. ' A System of Clauses ' 163.

... are a variety of hypothetical clauses ";[2] in the words of Wendt, the concessive sentence " ist, soweit es sich um seine potentiale oder irreale Bedeutung handelt, nur eine besondere Form bzw. begriffliche Schattierung des Konditionalsatzes."[3] Horn, too, points to the connection between the two relationships and notes that in Gothic (*jah*)*jabai* concession is expressed through conditional elements, while in *þauhjabai* the two relations are united; similarly there is the medieval German *ob*.[4] Later (p. 223), he draws attention to the union of concession and condition symbolized in the NE group ' as though.'

In OE this is illustrated by a rare concessive use of *gif*; thus in Gen 66I we read, ' Even though (*gif*) you spoke amiss, He will yet (*þeah*) forgive.' Here the dependent member postulates a condition not of the fulfillment of the main proposition but one despite which this proposition is valid.

The notional closeness of concession to exception is not usually remarked.[5] Yet, as we shall see below (III.6), Rübens (*Parataxe und Hypotaxe* 43) is capable of confusing one with the other, and our chief concessive sign in NE was in OE almost entirely confined to the expression of exception.

But closer than the connection between concession and condition or exception is that between concession and cause. Burnham shrewdly points out that concession " may often be looked upon as a blocked or inoperative cause "; this is true, she says, when " the reason, the circumstance is admitted, but the opposite of its natural consequence is asserted " (p. 2; she treats the connection more fully on pp. 112f.). Some grammarians, for example Mätzner and Poutsma, clearly reckon the connection with cause—or rather the dependence on cause—more fundamental than the connection with condition. Thus Mätzner has a general classification *Kausalverhältnis*, and as subsidiaries of this he ranks cause, condition, and concession;[6] Poutsma's system agrees with this.[7] Ohlander, who notes the difficulty of deciding at times whether ME *and* is concessive or causal (*Coordinate Expressions* 13), gives examples of *and*-members being concessive and causal at the same time: ' I meruail me, How þou to speke has swilk pouste And has na tong ne other thing, þat instrument es of spekyng.' Here, he says (p. 25), the *and*-member is in concessive relation with the pre-

---

2. *New English Grammar* I.§295; cf. also Wilmanns, III.I.260, and Jespersen ('System' 167f.) who seems almost to reach the point of identifying them.
3. *Syntax des heutigen Englisch* II.229.
4. 'Untersuchungen zur historischen englischen Syntax' 221.
5. Except in so far as exception is only a special case of condition; cf. Curme, *Syntax* 317f.
6. *Englische Grammatik* III.489ff.
7. *Late Modern English* I.Ch. XVII.

ceding *how*-member but in causal relation with the whole complex idea of marveling.

Lerch gives us an excellent table comparing cause, condition, and concession. He does so by distinguishing from ordinary concession a 'bedingtkonzessiv' relation (in the present study called 'even' concession), and presents the variations involved in a single relation, that of 'wealth' to 'marriageableness':

kausal:	*real-konzessiv:*
Da sie reich ist, heiratet er sie.	Obgleich sie reich ist, heiratet er sie nicht.
konditional:	*bedingt-konzessiv:*
Wenn sie reich wäre, würde er sie heiraten.	Wenn sie auch reich wäre, würde er sie doch nicht heiraten.[8]

According to this, condition is not directly related to ordinary concessions but to concessions of the 'even' type (see below), and cause is not directly related to all concessions but only to the ordinary or simple concessions. Nevertheless, not all simple concessions are equally close to a causal relationship. On the one hand we have

I'm not rich and yet I'm happy   (concession)
I'm rich and therefore I'm happy   (cause)

where the cause and the concession are obviously connected, the one being simply an inversion of the other; but although the concession in the following example is just as 'real,' it is not connected with an inverted cause in the same way:

She didn't come and yet I thought she would.

We shall find a good deal of interrelation between cause and concession in the OE material. One example will suffice; in the poetic version of the Boethian *Metres* we find a sentence containing a *þeah*-concession: 'The earth and sea cannot burn *though* they have fire in them' (Bo 20/114). In the prose version on which the poetic one is based we find that this sentence contains a causal *nu*-member: 'You have wrought it wonderfully so that fire cannot burn earth and water *now that* both contain fire.'

The only grammatical relation allied to concession which gives us real difficulty in practical analysis is the adversative. The points of contact between these two, and likewise the differences, have aroused the interest of many scholars, but because we are involved here with actual difficulties encountered in analyzing the present material, it

---

8. *Hist. franz. Synt.* II.333–4.

seems best to reserve discussion of the matter for the place where the problem first arises (III.2).

It remains to list briefly the different notional types of concessive relationship. First there is the so-called ' simple ' concession, on which sufficient has already been said; secondly, there is the ' alternative ' concession ('rain or shine, we leave today') which is discussed under this head in IV.2, followed shortly after by the third type, the ' indefinite ' concession ('whatever the weather, we leave today'). These three types are readily recognized and have been exhaustively handled in current grammars.

Less attention has been paid in the past to the fourth type, the ' even ' concession. In this, one part of an utterance introduces surprise which demonstrates that another part is inherently surprising; thus we read in ASC E 1086: 'A man might walk unharmed throughout the realm,—even laden with gold.' We find ' even ' concessions where we might have expected instead the expression of some limiting factor, as in, 'A man might walk unharmed throughout the realm, provided he had no gold in his pocket.'

In the present material some ' even ' concessions are expressed clearly, with as readily recognizable concessive forms as the Shakespearian ' What though . . . ? ' Often however we have to look closely at the function of special forms in relation to the whole context, since ' even ' concessions are often merely hinted. We may compare the modern colloquial expression ' So what? ' or the slight change that takes place in the following sentence on the introduction of an ' even ' concession:

> There is opportunity for much work on Chaucer.
> There is still opportunity for much work on Chaucer.

The phenomenon occurs in various forms throughout the material; see II.12, III.7, IV.20, 21.

The fifth type is the ' elliptical ' concession. Many scholars have gone wrong in their analysis of sentences like the following, quoted by Burnham, p. 4: 'He is an ingenious lad, though his brother is more ingenious.' The two members are obviously not in such a straightforward concessive relation as in ' He is an ingenious lad, though he looks stupid,' but one should hardly conclude that there is therefore no concession. Behaghel's analysis of such relations as elliptical concessions seems more accurate.[9] A discussion of the type appears below in II.11.

Finally, there are the ' concessive-equivalent ' constructions, embrac-

---

9. *Deutsche Syntax* III.§1422.

ing those concessions which are expressed through other relationships. It must be emphasized that this type has nothing to do with elements used or formerly used to express one relationship and capable of expressing concession without reference to the other relationship; thus *while* is a temporal element ('While the sun is shining, we can make hay') which can be used concessively without reference to time ('While the sun is shining, one cannot say it's very warm'). Concessive-equivalent constructions express the two relationships simultaneously, as in 'We sometimes look for praise *when we've done nothing to deserve it.*' This type is discussed further in iv.10.

3. PREVIOUS WORK ON OLD ENGLISH CONCESSION

Burnham's is the only previous monograph devoted to the problem of concession in OE, and there have been few other scholars who have made major contributions to the study. Several have written on individual points and constructions, and there have also been some surveys of the whole subject in the course of general studies in OE syntax. In the last category, we may mention (in chronological order) Kellner's *Historical Outlines of English Syntax*, which briefly relates OE to NE concessive constructions (§127 f.); and Western's *De Engelske Bisætninger, en Historisk-syntaktisk Studie*, which sketches the process by which *þeah* assumed connective function (pp. 12f.) and gives some notes on OE concessive constructions (p. 42). Wülfing's vast work, *Die Syntax in den Werken Alfreds des Grossen*, deals with concession in some detail and his abundant examples are useful, but his preoccupation with the question of mood in concession and his erratic criteria for distinguishing one mood from another limit the value of this study. Rübens' *Parataxe und Hypotaxe* is of interest in being among the earliest works to give prominence to the less formal aspects of concession (cf. especially pp. 8, 31). In his *Geschichte der englischen Sprache* (ii: *Historische Syntax*), Einenkel seeks to relate English to French constructions and thus tends to begin his work with ME; nevertheless, he has some interesting comments on the OE concessive constructions (p. 43f.). Trnka's somewhat neglected syntactical analysis of the language of OE poetry deals with concession only in passing, but his remarks are noteworthy in that he makes his analysis strictly in terms of the material in front of him; his work reminds us that a syntactical pattern is associated with specific forms of expression and cannot be assumed to be repeated with other forms. Finally, there is Mossé's brief account of dependent concessions in the first volume of *Manuel de l'Anglais du Moyen Age.* Among the scholars who have contributed studies which touch on individual aspects of OE concession, a few may be singled out for mention here. Morgan Callaway, in *The Absolute Participle in Anglo-Saxon,* ' The Appositive Participle in Anglo-Saxon,' and *Studies in the Syntax of the Lindisfarne Gospels,* lists the fairly rare functionally concessive OE participles. Mather's monograph on *The Conditional Sentence in Anglo-Saxon* contains valuable notes (pp. 21f.) on the interrelation of condition and concession in OE. Sarrazin's *Von Kädmon bis Kynewulf* is of interest here in that the author discusses certain concessive elements (particularly *þeah, hwæðere,* and *gyt*) in relation to dating criteria (see especially pp. 5, 30, 40, 117). Finally, there are Ericson's studies on OE *swa,* which established the essentially modal character of this element.

Although Schücking's *Die Grundzüge der Satzverknüpfung* is a general syntactical analysis of *Beowulf,* his handling of concession entitles this work to a place among the major contributions to this subject. Not only does the author deal with the theory of concession and with the ordinary *þeah* constructions, but for the first time considers the question of elliptical concession in *Beowulf* and also analyzes the challenge construction. He gives prominence to the adversative function of *ac* and distinguishes this from the annulling ('aufhebende') and causal functions; he discusses constructions with *hwæðere, no þy ær* and zero relating element; he even comments (in the footnotes to §15) on the possibility that the study of concession may throw light sociologically and anthropologically on the OE period, since concessions show what was obviously considered normal.

Second in point of date but first in importance comes Burnham's study. Her work is entirely confined to the concessive phenomena of the OE prose, and the material is classified as ' simple concessive clauses,' ' disjunctive concessive clauses,' ' indefinite concessions,' ' clauses of other kinds adapted to concessive use,' ' coördinate and juxtaposed clauses,' and ' phrases and single words used concessively.' Her survey has been recognized as sound; the phenomena are related at every point to current English usage, and her theoretical approach is for the most part clearly thought out and reliable. She has been criticized [1] for giving inadequate illustrations, and one might mention similarly her reluctance to give figures. She is also perhaps overcautious, tending to concentrate on texts which have a Latin original

---

1. Shearin, MLN xxvi.256.

to the neglect of forms of concession outside such texts and at the risk of giving undue prominence to Latin-influenced constructions. Her approach of course was not purely functional, and this is reflected in the attention devoted to *þeah*-concessions with the corresponding neglect of such nondependent concessions as those formed with *ac*. All the more praiseworthy, therefore, is her brilliant analysis, more than 40 years ago, of concessive-equivalent constructions.

In 1924 appeared R. A. Williams' *The Finn Episode in Beowulf*, where in addition to some comments of doubtful validity on the idiomatic use of *þeah* in *Beowulf* (pp. 88f.) he contributes the lengthiest study yet made of OE *ac* (pp. 48, 148–63). His theoretical approach is most valuable and much of the detailed application is sound and illuminating, but the study suffers from a too rigid desire to force his theory on every example. He attacks Schücking for an excessively doctrinaire approach, but it may be wondered whether his own is much less dogmatic.

Horn's 'Untersuchungen zur historischen englischen Syntax' is a study specifically of the use of *þeah* in OE, together with such discussion as seemed necessary on the nature of concession and its connection with the conditional relationship. It takes into account the cognate medieval German forms of concessive expression, inquires into the use of the subjunctive in dependent *þeah*-members, and looks forward from OE to the more modern functions of *though*. It is a useful study in its discussion and criticism of 19th-century work on the subjunctive, as well as in its partial collection of OE concessive data.

Glunz' monograph on *Die Verwendung des Konjunktivs im Altenglischen* was published in 1929. It deals with the concessive subjunctive at some length (pp. 52–68, 116–17), with a general discussion and something of a survey of previous work. The study is important for its handling of the 'challenge' nature of concession and for the case it makes for the use of the subjunctive having become formalized in late OE poetry and to a lesser extent in the prose as well. But Glunz' work is marred by two serious defects. He has no very clear idea of the limits of the concessive relation and interprets concession far too widely; moreover, he not only allows himself unreliable criteria for distinguishing one mood from another, but (p. 55) bases a general rule on forms which show that he fails to distinguish one tense from another.

His unreliability is criticized by Behre in *The Subjunctive in Old English Poetry*, who in contrast bases his " investigation exclusively upon determinate subjunctive forms " (p. 4). On the other hand his essential outlook and argument do not differ from those of Glunz: the subjunctive in concessive sentences is volitional but not in the sense that it is spontaneous and independent, since it is prompted only by the content of the other part of the sentence; it is in fact the volitional subjunctive modified into a challenge (p. 120).

Finally, there are Hans-Oskar Wilde's articles, published in 1939 and 1940, on 'Aufforderung, Wunsch und Möglichkeit,' which thoroughly analyze the mood and construction of the concessions with *þeah*, conditions with *gif*, and final clauses with *þæt* in a short selection of OE prose and poetic texts. Wilde, with his grasp of modern syntactical theory, corrects many of the misinterpretations of previous scholars; like Ericson, he concludes (pp. 330–31) that the concessive function of *swa* is a derived one, since *swa* is almost always fundamentally modal. In his general conclusion he is able to claim that *þeah* constructions have made the least progress of the three toward a valuable 'real—unreal' distinction in their use of the moods and toward a flexible use of periphrastic mood forms. Thus, he says, the concessive clause (*Konzessivsatz*) is a relatively late development in the language, and, unlike the conditional clause for example, is to a great extent confined to literary and learned usage. Wilde is referring of course only to dependent concessive clauses introduced by *þeah*, and since he is not concerned with concessions formed with *hwæðere* or *ac* or even with nondependent *þeah*-members, his remarks must not be construed as covering concession per se.

The importance of previous work on individual topics will appear below as these subjects come up for discussion. Thus for instance the use of the subjunctive is dealt with in II.7, the relation of 'parataxis,' 'coordination,' and 'hypotaxis' in III.12, the function of *all* in concessions in IV.2.

II

Concessions Formed with *þeah*

1. GENERAL

WHILE not more than a fifth of the concessions found in OE poetry are formed with *þeah*, this word must necessarily be given a primary position in any consideration of the concessive relation in OE. Like *hwæðere*, but few other elements, *þeah* is an explicit sign of concession and is almost exclusively confined to this relational function.[1]

In its various grammatical functions (conjunction, adversative adverb), phonetic and orthographic variants (such as *þeh, þæh*), and combinations (such as *þeah þe, swa þeah, þeahhwæðere*), *þeah* occurs as follows: Gen 21 times (17 in Gen B), Ex 6, Dan 11, ChrSat 3, And 16, Soul I 3, HomFrag I 2, El 14, Chr 10, Gl 20, Az 1, Ph 5, Jul 8, Wand 1, Prec 1, Seaf 2, Vain 1, Wid 1, Fort 1, Max I 3, Soul II 2, Rid 20, Jud I 1, Resig 9, Hell 1, HomFrag II 1, Husband 1, ParPs 19, Bo 67, Wald 2, Maldon 1, ASC Poems 2, Rune 6, Sol 5, Jud II 1, Exhort 1, Lord's Prayer II 1, Prayer 2, Leiden 2, Beo 32, Jud 2.

2. REINFORCEMENT AND CORRELATION

It is of interest first to note the ways in which other elements contribute to concessions formed with *þeah*. By *reinforcement* may be understood the multiple signaling of the concessive relation within a member, for example:

He went, *but* he was sorry *for all that*.
He went, *yet nevertheless* with regret.

Correlation on the other hand has to do with linking different members in a concessive relation:

---

1. Cf. Burnham, Ch. II; for MHG functions of *doch*, see Mensing, *Untersuchungen* 22f., 25f., and Kuhlmann, *Konzessivsätze* 10f.

Although he went, he was *nevertheless* sorry.
Though with regret, he went *all the same*.

Reinforcement is chiefly found in grammatically nondependent members of a relationship. For our purposes these are of three kinds and may be grouped in contrast to the grammatically dependent members:

1. A coordinated finite verb group in a compound sentence: 'He went, (*and*) *yet he was sorry.*'
2. A coordinated phrase: 'He went, (*and*) *yet regretfully.*'
3. A main clause correlated to a dependent clause or phrase: 'Although he went, *he was nevertheless sorry.*'

In OE poetry there are 95 nondependent members containing *þeah* (including 12 correlated and 5 phrase members), and in nearly two-thirds of these *þeah* is reinforced. The resulting reinforced groups almost all consist of or contain *swa þeah*, a typical example being:

Læddan þa leode   laðne gewinnan
to carcerne.   He wæs Criste swa þeah
leof on mode.   (And 1249)

swa þeah (or *seþeah*, e.g., Chr 209, *seþeana*, e.g., Gl 407, *swa þeana* e.g., Rid 58/12):

Gen 2390, Ex 337, Dan 580, And 811 (subordinating? See II.4), 1249, Soul I 65, El 494, Chr 209, 517, 1183, 1305, Gl 108, 407, 488, 939, 959, Ph 563, Fort 21, Max I 103, Soul II 60, Rid 58/10, 12, 87/6, 88/5, Resig 29, 46, 51, Bo 15/7, 19/5, 20/52, Jud II 57, Beo 970, 1925, 2964.

and(. . .)swa þeah:

HomFrag I 3 (MS: *ond . . . swa swa þeah*), Bo 11/43, DeathEdward 25, Beo 2877.

ac . . . swa þeah:

ParPs 88/28.

efne swa þeah:

Hell 118, Rune 51; *efne seþeah*: Rid 39/27, 65/1; *emne swa þeah*: Bo 9/34.

hwæðere swa þeah:

Beo 2441; *hwæþre seþeah*: Rid 35/9 (*huethrae suae ðeh*: Leiden 9).

swa þeah hwæðere:

ParPs 118/157.

hwæðere þeah:

Bo 20/52, 229.

ðeh hwæðre:

Sol 440.

ðeah gita:

Bo 23/1.

and(. . .)*þeah*:

Dan 513, Bo 2/8, 7/14, 10/14, 13/6, 20/136, 157, 28/37, Rune 87.

These phenomena are closely paralleled in prose usage, as we may see from Burnham, pp. 29–30.

Finally, an example of unreinforced *þeah* in a nondependent member:

Wæs gehwæðeres waa.
Þeah wæs magorinca   mod mid Grecum   (Bo 1/25)

Although reinforcement is a feature chiefly of nondependent members, it occurs occasionally in dependent members too. The subordinating conjunction *þeah* is reinforced by *nu* in Bo 16/8 (2x), 22/25, and by *nu geta* in Bo 24/44. In El 1120 we find *ær* similarly used with *þeah*, and in Soul I 135 *gyt* reinforces the conjunction *þeah ðe* (though here the conjunction itself is an emendation; MS: 'ahðæ'). Note also the function of the *ofer*-phrase in Prec 70:

ne habbað wiht for þæt,   þeah hi wom don
ofer meotudes bibod.

Evidence for the rise of 'although,' a special case of reinforcement, can best be discussed later along with other concessive functions of 'all' (see IV.23).

Correlation is chiefly found linking dependent and nondependent members, and in OE several different elements in the nondependent members are used to correlate with subordinating *þeah* (*þe*) in the dependent members. Indeed, there are so many that an analysis of concessive correlation in OE may become very subjective as one passes from the unquestionable examples into classes of possible or suspected examples.[2] Care is taken in the following list, therefore, to avoid all dubious cases of correlation, even at the risk of making the survey incomplete.

2. The position is similar in the prose; see Burnham, pp. 30–2.

þeah . . . þeah:

    Dependent member first: Bo 10/7, 15/1, 20/125, 146.
    Dependent member second: Bo 20/63.

There are two other examples of *þeah* used correlatively with a dependent concessive member, one introduced by *swa*, the other by *gif*:

                    swa he us ne mæg ænige synne gestælan,
    þæt we him . . . lað gefremedon,   he hæfð us þeah þæs leohtes
                                        bescyrede   (Gen 391)
    Gif þu him heodæg wuht   hearmes gespræce,
    he forgifð hit þeah   (Gen 661)

þeah (þe) . . . swa þeah (or *seþeah, seþeana*):

    Chr 1183, Ph 563, Resig 46, 51.
    Dependent member second: Resig 29.

þeah (þe) . . . hwæðere:

    Dan 232, Ph 638, Jul 515, ParPs 77/21, and (according to R. W. Chambers' interpretation, which we shall consider below in II.6) Beo 1713.
    Dependent member second: And 48, Jud 1 98, Resig 25.
    Gen 952 has the double correlative pattern 'hwæðre . . . þeah þe . . . hwæðere':

        No hwæðre ælmihtig   ealra wolde
        Adame and Euan   arna ofteon,
        fæder æt frymðe,   þeah þe *hie him from swice,
        ac he him to frofre let   hwæðere forð wesan
        hyrstedne hrof   halgum tunglum
                              *MS: he

The following correlations, all with the dependent member second unless otherwise stated, are sporadic but no less valid; the number of temporal elements involved is noteworthy:

swa . . . þeah:

    Gen 733: 'Swa þu . . . ne þearft . . . murnan on mode . . . þeah wit hearmas nu . . . þoliað.'

huru . . . þeah þe:

        Huru þæt on lande   lyt manna ðah
        mægenagendra   mine gefræge,
        þeah ðe he dæda gehwæs   dyrstig wære   (Beo 2836)

nu . . . þeah (þe):

    Fyl nu þa frumspræce,   þeah þe user fea lifgen   (Az 42)

So too El 1120. Note that *nu* also plays a part in the *þeah . . . þeah* correlation of Bo 15/1.

Dependent member first:

    Wine leofesta,   *þeah *ðe wyrmas gyt
    gifre gretaþ,   nu is þin gast cumen
                  *MS: ahðæ   (Soul 1 135)

nu gyt (or *gen*) *. . . þeah:*

  Gen 1037: '. . . nu giet, þeah . . .'
  And 474: '. . . nu gena . . . þeah . . .'

þa gen . . . þeah þe:

  Gl 515; cf. And 48: 'Hwæðre . . . þa git . . . þeah ðe . . .'

gen . . . þeah:

                Gen ic feores þe
    unnan wille,   þeah þu ær fela
    unwærlicra   worda gespræce   (Jul 191)

Compare Beo 583: 'næfre git . . . þeah . . .'

þonne . . . þeah:

    Đonne wene ic to þe   wyrsan geþingea,
    ðeah þu heaðoræsa   gehwær dohte   (Beo 525)

Finally, there is an important class in which *þeah (þe)* in the dependent member correlates with a negative statement containing *þy* and a comparative. Ex 259 provides an example:

    Ne beoð ge þy forhtran,   þeah þe Faraon brohte
    sweordwigendra   side hergas,
    eorla unrim!

Other examples are:

  Dan 753: 'ne ðy hraðor . . . ðeah ðe . . .'
  Rid 13/5: 'Ne . . . þy wyrs . . . þeah . . .'
  Bo 15/10: 'þeah . . . næron hy ðy weorðran . . .'
  Beo 2160, 2466: 'no ðy ær . . . þeah . . .'[3]

Compare also (especially with Ex 259):

    Ne beoð ge to forhte,   þeh þe fell curen
    synnigra cynn.   (And 1609)

---

3. Cf. Andrew, *Syntax and Style* 70f., and see below, III.12, IV.17.

In Bo the nondependent member is sometimes a question rhetorically equal to a negative statement. For example:

> Þeah ge nu wenen   and wilnigen
> þæt ge lange tid   libban moten,
> hwæt iow æfre þy bet   bio oððe þince?   (Bo 10/63)

The other instances are:

Bo 14/1: 'Hwæt . . . ðe bet, þeah . . .'
Bo 15/13: 'Ðeah . . . hu . . . ðy selra . . .'
Bo 16/8: 'Þeah . . . hwy . . . þy mara . . .'

In some cases, the original prose version similarly has the question form. Thus, corresponding to Bo 10/63, the prose reads:

> Þeah ge nu wenen 7 wilnian þ ge lange libban scylan her on worulde, hwæt bið eow þōn þy bet?

Correlation between nondependent *þeah*-members is rare and the only examples come from Bo:

swa þeah . . . þeah:

> Hwæt, se feond swa ðeah
> his diorlingas   duguðum stepte.
> Ne mæg ic þeah gehycgan   hwy him on hige þorfte
> a ðy sæl wesan   (Bo 15/7)

þeah . . . þeah:

Bo 20/164.

hwæðere þeah . . . swa þeah:

Bo 20/52.

3. WORD ORDER IN NONDEPENDENT MEMBERS

Analysis shows that the position of *þeah* and *þeah*-groups in nondependent members bears no relation to whether they are correlated with *þeah* (*þe*) in a dependent member or not; all nondependent members may therefore be grouped together for the purpose of considering their word order. Nor does the actual form of the *þeah*-group apparently influence its position in the member. Indeed the bewildering variety of *þeah*-groups and of positions they take up makes only one general conclusion possible, namely, that *initial* position for any group is on the whole rarer than a relatively posterior position, although initial position is the commonest one in Bo. The survey in some detail is as follows:

(*swa*) *þeah* initially:

And 811, El 494, Ph 563, Bo 1/25, 10/7, 15/1, 20/125, 146, 22/35, Wald II 22.

and (*swa*) *þeah:*

Dan 513, Bo 2/8, 7/14, 11/31, 43, 13/6, 20/136, 157, 28/37, Rune 87.

The total in these two sections is 20, and the word order within the member is fairly evenly divided between *subject–verb* and *verb–subject*.

Subject–(*swa*) *þeah–verb–etc.* (*etc.–verb:* Bo 15/7, 20/164):

Gen 558, 824, HomFrag I 3, Chr 1088, Gl 939, Rid 4/7, 87/6, Resig 29, ParPs 88/28, Bo 10/10, DeathEdward 25, Jud II 57, Beo 970. Total: 15.

verb–(*swa*) *þeah–subject–etc:*

Dan 211, 237, 574, Chr 517, Rid 58/10, Bo 20/63, 22/43, 31/10, Rune 1, 51 (*efne swa ðeah*), 59, Beo 2441 (*hwæðre swa þeah*), Jud 253.
Total: 13.

subject–verb–(*swa*) *þeah–etc.:*

Gen 391, 704, 719, And 1249, Chr 1183 (subject zero), Gl 108, 407 (subject zero), Max I 103, Rid 58/12 (subject zero), Bo 19/5, 20/52 (*hwæðre þeah*; subject and verb zero), 55 (subject zero), 142, 166 (subject zero), 229 (*hwæðre þeah*; subject and verb zero), 23/1, 26/95, Maldon 288, Sol 440 (*ðeh hwæðre*; subject and auxiliary verb zero), Beo 2877 (subject zero).
Total: 20.

verb–subject–(*swa*) *þeah–etc.:*

Gen 359, 2390, Soul I 65, Chr 1305, Soul II 60, Rid 35/9 (*hwæþre seþeah*; Leiden 9: *huethrae suae ðeh*), Resig 46, 51, Hell 118 (*efne swa þeah*), ParPs 118/157 (*swa þeah hwæðere*), Bo 9/34 (*emne swa þeah*), 15/9, 30/5, Rune 27, Beo 1925, 2964.
Total: 17.

(*swa*) *þeah* in final position:

Gen 661, Ex 337, Dan 124, Chr 209 (phrase only), Gl 488, 959, Fort 21, Rid 6/6, 39/27 (*efne seþeah*), 65/1 (*efne seþeah*).
Total: 10, the word order *subject–verb* predominating.

Finally, there is one example (Rid 88/5) where the manuscript is too defective for us to know the details of word order.

Burnham gives no corresponding data for the prose, but an analysis of ASC and part of Oros shows that the word order there is equally free and that all possible variations occur.

4. THE SUBORDINATING CONJUNCTION

As a subordinating conjunction in the poetry þeah appears both alone and in company with the particle þe. This is true also of the prose (Burnham, pp. 12f.). In addition, it may be possible to interpret swa þeah in And 811 as subordinating. This þeah-group seems to occur in subordinating function in Gothic (sveþauh, 2 Cor.12.15) and Burnham (pp. 16–7) produces scattered examples in OE prose. Usually it has the form swa þeah þe, but she finds the simpler form used in a dependent phrase in Ælfric's *Homilies* (1.2):

> Ic Ælfric munuc and mæssepreost, swa þeah waccre þonne swilcum hadum gebyrige, wearð asend . . .

The dubious example from the poetry is as follows:

> Nu ðu miht gehyran, hyse leofesta,
> hu he wundra worn wordum cyðde,
> swa þeah ne gelyfdon larum sinum
> modblinde menn.   (And 811)

As we shall see from the section on mood below (II.7), a determinate subjunctive form of the verb would have been decisive, but in view of the indeterminate form of *gelyfdon* and of there being no parallel examples in the corpus of poetry, it is safest to reckon swa þeah as adverbial in a nondependent member.

Burnham (p. 18) also cites þeah hwæðere and swa þeah hwæðere as possible subordinating conjunctions in the prose, but the single example of each quoted hardly seems to justify this interpretation.

Much importance has been attached to the distribution of þeah and þeah þe as subordinating conjunctions, particularly by scholars interested in the genetic study of dependent clauses.[4] As there has hitherto been no extensive examination of the distribution, figures are given below showing the use of these two forms of the conjunction in the poetic texts:[5]

---

4. See particularly Horn, 'Untersuchungen zur hist. engl. Syntax' 217f., Western, *De Engelske Bisætninger* 13.
5. The figures for the prose of ASC are: þeah 22, þeah þe 4.

	Gen	Ex	Dan	ChrSat	And	Soul I
beah	11 (B: 10)	1	1	3	11	1
beah þe	2	4	5	—	3	?1 (MS: ahðæ)

	HomFrag I	El	Chr	Gl	Az	Ph
beah	1	12	5	9	—	4
beah þe	—	1	—	6	1	—

	Jul	Wand	Prec	Seaf	Vain	Wid
beah	5 (1 *þa*?)	—	1	—	—	—
beah þe	3	1	—	2	1	1

	Max I	Soul II	Rid	Jud I	Resig	HomFrag II
beah	2	1	8	—	1	1
beah þe	—	—	3	1	5	—

	Husband	ParPs	Bo	Wald	ASC Poems	Rune
beah	—	1	35	—	—	1
beah þe	1	16	2	1	1	—

	Sol 1	Sol 2	Exhort	Lord's Prayer II	Prayer	Leiden
beah	1	1	1	1	2	—
beah þe	1	1	—	—	—	1

	Beo	Jud	Totals
beah	12	1	134
beah þe	15	—	79

It will be seen that each poem, apart notably from Beo, Gl, and Jul, seems to favor one particular form of the conjunction—though not normally to the complete exclusion of the other. In view of the OS use of *thoh* alone as a subordinating conjunction, it is interesting to note that Gen B has 10 instances of *þeah* in this function and none of *þeah þe*.

The possibility of a relation between the incidence of *þeah–þeah þe* and other dual features will be discussed in II.14.

5. WORD ORDER IN DEPENDENT MEMBERS

As in the prose (Burnham, pp. 18–19), the subordinating conjunction stands at the head of the dependent member:

                           Heo þæs beornes lufan
fæste wiðhogde,   þeah þe feohgestreon
under hordlocan,   hyrsta unrim
æhte ofer eorþan.   (Jul 41)

The only poetic exception is in Rid 48/1:

    Ic gefrægn *for hæleþum   hring endean,
    torhtne butan tungan,   tila þeah he hlude
    stefne ne cirmde,   strongum wordum.
        *MS: fer

'Well though he cried not' has a pattern which was certainly flourishing in early ME: "'þeah' frequently takes second place, e. g., soð þeih hit nere ..."[6] But in the present instance it would be easier to demonstrate that the member was dependent if we had *þeah þe* instead of *þeah* or a determinate subjunctive verb instead of *cirmde*. Even so, however, the member seems genuinely dependent; the pattern is not paralleled among the nondependent members we have analyzed, and from the logical point of view (though this is not a reliable criterion, as we shall see below in II.7) the member should be dependent. Moreover, although this type of disjunction is rare in OE, it can be paralleled in the prose (see Burnham, p. 19). Its rarity in OE has led to the suggestion that it arises as a result of the influence of French on the syntax of English. "Da im AE. Entsprechendes, ausser dem einen Belege *uncuð þeah ic wære, ðonan cume ic to þæt ic etc.* Solil., sich nicht findet, so ist auch der reich entwickelte afrz. Gebrauch zum

---

6. Bøgholm, *The Layamon Texts* 84.

Vergleiche heranzuziehen. Die gewöhnlichsten Fälle sind: afrz. *E trop large, Li prie, que ele n'en soit* Chev. au Lyon > me. *Betere him were, iborin þat he nere* Rel.Ant. > *þa com his lifes ende, lað þah him were* Laȝ . . ."[7]

Before leaving this subject, one might perhaps mention cases where *þeah* only apparently fails to take initial position. There are examples in which the *þeah*-member as a whole is really placed medially in the sentence but with only one word of the surrounding nondependent member placed initially. This pattern seems to occur especially where *þeah* means '*even* though.' For example:

> Ne þeah engla werod   up on heofenum
> snotra tosomne   sæcgan ongunnon,
> ne magon hy næfre areccean,   ne þæt gerim wytan,
> hu þu mære eart,   mihtig drihten.   (Prayer 35)

As with the position of *þeah*, so with the order of words within the dependent member there is fundamental agreement between the poetry and the prose. There is clearly a *regular* word order, which is unaffected by whether the dependent member precedes or follows its nondependent member; it is *subject–object/complement–verb*. There seems to be stricter adherence to this pattern in the prose than in the verse, but even in the poetic material the regular order is found in about two-thirds of the cases.[8] For example:

> Ic his word oncneow,
> þeh he his mægwlite   bemiðen hæfde.   (And 855)

We must add some minor qualifications. 'Variation,' for example, sometimes forces a slight departure from the regular order:

> A wæs *secg oð ðæt
> cnyssed cearwelmum, **h** drusende,
> þeah he in medohealle   maðmas þege,
> æplede gold.   *MS: sæcc   (El 1256)
> Ðonne wene ic to þe   wyrsan geþingea,
> ðeah þu headoræsa   gehwær dohte,
> grimre guðe   (Beo 525)

Compare also Beo 583, 1368.

A similar departure occurs when the subject, part of the object or complement group, and the verb fit into the second half line culminating

---

7. Einenkel, *Geschichte der englischen Sprache* II.187.
8. Except in Bo, where the generally more involved syntax yields this order in only two-fifths of the examples.

CONCESSIONS FORMED WITH þeah II.5

in the verb, and the rest of the object or complement group follows in the next first half line. For example:

>   Min is nu þa
> sefa synnum fah,   ond ic ymb sawle eom
> feam siþum forht,   þeah þu me fela sealde
> arna on þisse eorþan.   (Resig 64)

Sometimes the order is technically broken by an auxiliary verb following its subject closely but with the infinitive or participle concluding the member and thus making the pattern feel regular nevertheless. For example:

> Him se eadga wer   ageaf ondsware,
> leof mon leofum,   þeah he late meahte,
> eorl ellenheard,   oreþe gebredan   (Gl 1163)
> Næs nan þæs stronglic *stan gefæstnod,
> þeah he wære mid irne   eall ymbfangen
>   *MS: satan   (ChrSat 515)

Apart from the regular order and these modifications of it, we find almost every other possible variation of word order, but the commonest arrangement outside the regular one is undoubtedly *subject—verb—object/complement*. Thus: Dan 753, El 1120, Gl 380, Ph 563, Jul 494, 510, Wand 1, Max I 112, Soul II 71, Rid 13/5, 40/27, ParPs 128/5, 146/11, Bo 7/34, 14/1, 15/10, 22/25, Beo 1129 (subject zero), 1166, 2217, 2855. For example:

>   þeah hi sume hwile
> gecure butan cræftum   cyninga dysegast,
> næron hy ðy weorðran   witena ænegum.   (Bo 15/10)

As for the minor irregular groupings, it is necessary to give only a selection of examples:

object—verb—subject: e.g., And 1609, Seaf 97, Rune 81.

> Þeah þe græf wille   golde stregan
> broþor his geborenum   (Seaf 97)

verb—subject—object: e.g., Bo 13/39:

>   þeah him wolde hwilc
> heora lareowa   listum beodan
> þone ilcan mete

object—subject—verb—complement: e.g., Rid 40/46, Bo 15/13.

> Ðeah hine se dysega   do to cyninge   (Bo 15/13)

That these departures from the regular order are not entirely due to the difficulties of versifying is shown by the fact that we find the order *subject—verb—object/complement* occurring, for example, in Oros 21/15 and ASC E 1055, and the prose corresponding to Bo 22/25 has this order like its verse derivative. Indeed it is not very easy to demonstrate that the actual process of versifying led to irregularities of word order. Bo is the only text which provides evidence of the process, and when its dependent *þeah*-members correspond at all to those in the prose they usually retain the original order, the requirements of the new medium being met simply by substituting a word here and there for a synonym more suitable for the alliteration or meter; thus in Bo 7/50 *swence* for *blawe*, 10/10 ' þeah hio unwisum widgel þince ' for ' þeah heo us rum þince,' 10/24 *gesæle* for *gebyrige*; sometimes no change is necessary and the whole line Bo 10/63, for example, reads exactly as the prose: ' þeah ge nu wenen and wilnigen.' Occasionally too, as in Bo 13/51, the irregular order in the verse is less irregular than in the prose. In a couple of instances, however, where the prose has normal *subject–object–verb* order, the poetry substitutes *object–subject–verb* (Bo 15/1, 13), quite clearly for metrical reasons; minor adjustments in the order have been similarly caused in 13/35, 39.

6. THE PLACE OF DEPENDENT *þeah*-MEMBERS IN THE SENTENCE

In the poetry the overwhelming majority of dependent *þeah*-members follow the nondependent members with which they are in concessive relation; thus, in ParPs 113/16: ' Ne cleopigað hi care, þeah þe hi ceolan habban.' Most of the poetic texts have only scattered examples—if any at all—of departure from this pattern.[9] The dependent *þeah*-member takes front position, for example, in Dan 232, ChrSat 431, Soul 1 135 (if the usual emendation is accepted), El 393, Jul 397, Seaf 97, Max 1 112, Rid 40/27, 95/10, Resig 51, Sol 70, Exhort 22, Prayer 30, Beo 1368, the latter reading:

> Ðeah þe hæðstapa   hundum geswenced,
> heorot hornum trum   holtwudu sece,

---

9. According to Burnham (p. 26), dependent members follow and precede nondependent members fairly equally; this conclusion may be the result of not distinguishing between original OE prose and translations; certainly in ASC only 3 out of 26 members do not follow their related nondependent members.

> feorran geflymed, ær he feorh seleð,
> aldor on ofre, ær he in wille [1]

In ParPs, 4 out of 17 *þeah*-members precede the nondependent members, and 4 works have a fairly high proportion of this order; Gl has 5 out of 15, Chr 2 out of 5, Bo 19 out of 37 and Ph 4 out of 5. For example:

> Þeah þe ge me deað gehaten,
> mec wile wið þam niþum genergan se þe eowrum nydum
> wealdeð. (Gl 240)

> þeah hi wel sien,
> tela atemede, gif hi on treowum weorðað
> holte tomiddes, hræðe bioð forsewene
> heora lareowas, þe hi lange ær
> tydon and temedon. (Bo 13/35)

> Þeah min lic scyle
> on moldærne molsnad weorþan
> wyrmum to willan, swa þeah weoruda god
> æfter swylthwile sawle alyseð
> ond in wuldor aweceð. (Ph 563)

Medial position for the *þeah*-member is much rarer, but it is found, for example, in Gen 531, And 271, Jul 494, Bo 10/66, 18/5, 30/9. Thus:

> Ic asecgan ne mæg,
> þeah ic gesitte sumerlongne dæg,
> eal þa earfeþu þe ic ær ond siþ
> gefremede to facne (Jul 494)

Beo has a rather high proportion with 3 out of 12 (1612, 1830, and 2855), especially if we consider in this connection members which, while not grammatically medial, are notionally so. For example, Beo 525:

> Ðonne wene ic to þe wyrsan geþingea,
> ðeah þu heaðoræsa gehwær dohte,
> grimre guðe, gif þu Grendles dearst
> nihtlongne fyrst nean bidan.

Compare also Beo 2836.

The considerable regularity revealed here is of the greatest importance, not only in tracing the influence of Latin on OE, but also in deciding the punctuation and interpretation of difficult passages.

---

1. Note that Klaeber, ed. p. 184, says of this passage, "The elegant period might put us in mind of Vergil."

Cases in point are Jul 216, Chr 367, Gl 1064, 479, the latter reading, according to the punctuation in ASPR:

> Ne cunnon ge dryhten   duguþe biddan,
> ne mid eaðmedum   are secan,
> þeah þe eow alyfde   lytle hwile,
> þæt ge min onwald   agan mosten;
> ne ge þæt geþyldum   þicgan woldan,
> ac mec yrringa   up gelædon

Gollancz (*Exeter Book* 132) and Kennedy (*Poems of Cynewulf* 277) are prominent among those who take the *þeah þe* member with the lines that follow, whereas our analysis supports the interpretation which the ASPR punctuation suggests. A better known example of this type of difficulty exists in Beo 1713ff. where Klaeber reads:

> breat bolgenmod   beodgeneatas,
> eaxlgesteallan,   oþ þæt he ana hwearf,
> mære þeoden   mondreamum from,
> ðeah þe hine mihtig God   mægenes wynnum,
> eafeþum stepte,   ofer ealle men
> forð gefremede.   Hwæþere him on ferhþe greow
> breosthord blodreow;   nallas beagas geaf
> Denum æfter dome

Instead of the double concession of Klaeber's interpretation, Chambers makes only one concession with *ðeah þe* correlative to *hwæþere* and puts a period after *from* in 1715. As we have seen, so far as syntax is concerned, Klaeber's view is preferable.

7. MOOD IN CONCESSIVE SENTENCES CONTAINING *þeah*

All grammarians who have written on the concessive relation have devoted considerable attention to the part played in it by the subjunctive mood; it is almost equally true to say that all writers on the subjunctive stress the fact that this mood is fundamental in dependent concessive members. Hans-Oskar Wilde ('Aufforderung' 297) has restated the view that in IE we can distinguish fundamentally subjunctive types of relationship (for example, concession) from fundamentally indicative types (for example, cause). In coming to deal with PG *þauh*, he supports Behaghel's conclusion (*Syntax* III.1296) that just as *þauh* in the older Germanic syntax took the subjunctive, which doubtless arose

" aus einem auffordernden Optativ," so in OE *þeah* regularly took the subjunctive until after 1150 when the indicative crept in (op.cit.355).

Nevertheless, a number of scholars—among them Delbrück [2]—have been at pains to demonstrate that *þeah* does not necessarily take the subjunctive. Instances are cited from OE and OHG to show that the subjunctive is not essential to concession, but above all scholars point to Gothic to prove their point.[3] In the case of OE, Wülfing is particularly notable for his demonstration of the use of *þeah* with the indicative, filling two pages with examples of concessions so formed.[4] Thirty years after Wülfing we find Glunz repeating that it is mistaken to claim that concession and the subjunctive mood are inseparable. He too lists many examples of *þeah* taking the indicative, including several from *Beowulf*.[5] Both of these scholars, however, are uncritical of both material and criteria. Wülfing (§459) cites many examples, but in all cases except one we find that he is accepting the preterite plural endings *-on* and *-an* as evidence of indicative mood. His only example of an indisputably indicative form is from the prose Boethius: ' ac ic wolde . . . mare gehyran, þeah ðu nu hwene ær sædest,' but this is the reading of the late Bodleian manuscript; Sedgefield (50/22) printing the inflection from the Cotton manuscript has the subjunctive form *sæde*. Glunz, too, is guilty of giving indeterminate forms among his genuine indicative examples.[6]

Before we analyze the mood of *þeah*-concessions, it is therefore necessary to state definitely the principles on which the analysis is based. Clearly, we must avoid using the *distinction between unstressed vowels alone* as a criterion. Even in texts where there is some evidence that *-en* is confined to subjunctive endings and *-on* to indicative ones, I have declined to use this distinction, and *curen, curan, curon* (pret.pl.) have all been counted as indeterminate forms.[7] The unstressed vowel alone is, however, used as evidence of the mood when the opposition is *unstressed vowel–zero*, as in the 1st and 3d pers.sg.pret. of strong verbs: *for–fore, heold–heolde, het–hete*. Elsewhere, the distinction rests on the stressed vowel (*bat–bite, sceal–scyle*), on consonant alternation (*wæs–wære, doð–do, bindað–binden, bundon–bunde* [8]), or on distinct mood forms (*is–sie, sy*).

In the nondependent members containing *þeah* there is not of course

---

2. See especially PBBeit xxix.301, and cf. Horn's criticism in ' Untersuchungen ' 214–15.
3. For example, Wilmanns, *Deutsche Grammatik* III.I.260–1.
4. *Syntax in den Werken Alfreds* §460.
5. *Die Verwendung des Konjunktivs* 57–8.
6. See Behre's criticism in *Subjunctive in Old English Poetry* 122.
7. Cf. Horn, ' Untersuchungen ' 214.
8. Cf. Bloomfield, ' Old English Plural Subjunctives in *e* ' 100ff.

the slightest evidence of the subjunctive, but dependent members present a very different picture. The total number of finite verbs in members subordinated by *þeah* (*þe*) is 223; 127 of these are clearly subjunctive, 87 are indeterminate, and 9 are indicative. The detailed figures for the individual texts are as follows:

GEN SUBJ: 9 (in one case, *þeah* is nonconcessive). There are: 2x 2 p.sg.pres. forms, 2x 3 p.sg.pres., 4x 3 p.sg.pret., 1x 3 p. pl.pret. determined by omission of -*n*.
INDET: 3.
INDIC: 1. 1 p.pl.pres:'*þeah wit . . . þoliað*' 736. The indic. form is in Gen B, which has besides 7 subj. and 2 indet. forms.
EX INDET: 5, in one case because the text is deficient.
DAN SUBJ: 3. 2x 3 p.sg.pret., 1x 3 p.pl.pres.
INDET: 3.
CHRSAT SUBJ: 2. 1x 3 p.sg.pres., 1x 3 p.sg.pret.
INDET: 1.
AND SUBJ: 5. 1x 3 p.sg.pret., 1x 1 p.pl.pres., 2x 2 p.sg.pres., 1x 3 p.pl.pres.
INDET: 9.
SOUL 1 INDET: 1.
INDIC: 1. 3 p.pl.pres: ' *þeah *ðe wyrmas . . . gretaþ' 135; *MS: ahðæ.
HOMFRAG 1 SUBJ: 1. 3 p.sg.pres.
EL SUBJ: 6. 3x 3 p.sg.pret., 1x 1 p.pl.pres., 1x 3 p.pl.pres., 1x 1 p.sg.pret.
INDET: 7.
CHR SUBJ: 1. 1 p.pl.pres.
INDET: 3.
INDIC: 1. 3 p.sg.pret: '*þeah wæs hyre mægdenhad*' 1419.
GL SUBJ: 12. 6x 2 p.sg.pres., 2x 3 p.sg.pres., 2x 3 p.sg.pret., 1x 1 p.sg.pret., 1x 3 p.pl.pret. (omits -*n*).
INDET: 3.
AZ SUBJ: 1. 3 p.pl.pres.
PH SUBJ: 3. 2x 3 p.sg.pres., 1x 3 p.sg.pret.
INDET: 1.
JUL SUBJ: 3. 2x 3 p.sg.pres., 1x 3 p.sg.pret.
INDET: 4.
INDIC: 1. 1 p.sg.pret: '*þeah ic . . . slog*' 492.
WAND INDET: 1.
PREC SUBJ: 1. 3 p.pl.pres.
SEAF INDET: 2.
VAIN INDET: 1.

Wid Indet: 1.
Max i Subj: 2. 3 p.sg. pres.
Soul ii Indet: 1.
Rid Subj: 4. 3x 3 p.sg.pres., 1x 3 p.sg.pret.
    Indet: 6 (2 because text deficient).
    Indic: 1. 3 p.pl.pres: 'þeah nu ælda bearn . . . secað' 95/10.
Jud i Subj: 1. 3 p.sg.pres.
Resig Subj: 1. 2 p.sg.pret. (weak verb).
    Indet: 4.
HomFrag ii Subj: 1. 3 p.sg.pret.
Husband Indet: 1.
    Indic: 1. 3 p.sg.pret: 'þeah þe . . . min wine . . . aþrong' 39.
ParPs Subj: 14. 8x 3 p.pl.pres., 6x 3 p.sg.pres.
    Indet: 6.
Bo Subj: 35. 25x 3 p.sg.pres., 4x 3 p.pl.pres., 2x 2 p.sg.pres., 2x 2 p.pl.pres., 1x 3 p.sg.pret., 1x 3 p.pl.pret. (omits -n).
    Indet: 6.
    Indic: 1. 3 p.sg.pret: 'þeah hit . . . heold and hydde' 29/52.
Wald Indet: 1.
DeathEdward Indet: 1.
Rune Subj: 1. 3 p.pl.pres.
Sol Subj: 2. 3 p.sg.pres.
Exhort Subj: 2. 2 p.sg.pres.
Lord's Prayer ii Indet: 2.
Prayer Subj: 1. 3 p.sg.pres.
    Indet: 1.
Leiden Subj: 1. 3 p.sg.pres.
Beo Subj: 15. 8x 3 p.sg.pres., 6x 3 p.sg.pret., 1x 1 p.sg.pres. (mæge).
    Indet: 11 (1 because text deficient).
    Indic: 2. 3 p.sg.pret: 'þeh he þær monige geseah' 1613, 'þeah him leof ne wæs' 2467.
Jud Indet: 1.

It will be seen that the mood of verbs in dependent *þeah*-members is overwhelmingly subjunctive, and it is necessary now to look more closely at the exceptional instances of the indicative. Although the figure of nine cases was given, this needs qualification. To begin with, we must rule out the example in Jul 490 where the manuscript as it stands seems to make nonsense:

                Sume, þa ic funde
    butan godes tacne,   gymelease,
    ungebletsade,   þeah ic bealdlice

> þurh mislic cwealm   minum hondum
> searoþoncum slog.

Gollancz (*Exeter Book*) retains the manuscript reading, translating *þeah* as 'nevertheless,' and von der Warth [9] defends this interpretation, but most editors emend *þeah* to *þa* and would agree with Strunk's downright assertion that "It is not possible to make good sense out of the reading of the MS." [1] It is perhaps possible that the fiend kills off these sinners although there is no need (in view of their unregenerate character), and this is no doubt Gollancz' approach; but the *bealdlicc* is inconvenient for this view because it seems to imply a distinction between the fiend's attitude to the sinners and his more circumspect approach to the virtuous. In any case, even accepting *þeah* as concessive, it would seem more likely to belong to a nondependent than to a dependent member, and so on any count we must dismiss the indicative in this instance.

Secondly, the indicative form in Soul 1 135 is little more reliable, depending as it does upon emendation, albeit an attractive one:

> Wine leofesta,   *þeah *ðe wyrmas gyt
> gifre gretaþ,   nu is þin gast cumen
>   *MS: ahðæ [2]

Nor can the indicative in Husband 35 be accepted entirely without misgiving, because the fragmentary nature of the text makes it possible (though unlikely) that the indicative form in question is not in the dependent member introduced by *þeah þe*:

>   he genoh hafað
> fædan gold(.)s   (...................
> ....)d elþeode   eþel healde,
> fægre foldan   (....................
> .....)ra hæleþa,   þeah þe her min wine
>   (..................)
> nyde gebæded,   nacan ut aþrong,
> ond on yþa geong   (....) sceolde
> faran on flotweg [3]

It is probably right to assume that both *aþrong* and *sceolde* are in dependent members introduced by the *þeah þe*, but the possibility that

---

9. *Metrisch-sprachliches und Textkritisches zu Cynewulfs Werken* (Halle 1908) 39.
1. *Juliana* (Boston 1904) 56.
2. The only other emendation worthy of note is the unsatisfactory *agon ðe* 'possess thee' suggested by L. F. Klipstein, *Analecta Anglo-Saxonica* (New York 1849) II.135.
3. Points within parentheses indicate the probable number of letters missing.

the gap following *wine* contained the conclusion of the *þeah*-member cannot be excluded.

There are no textual difficulties with the passage beginning at Chr 1418, but doubts may well be entertained as to whether the *þeah*-member is dependent or not:

>Þa ic sylf gestag,
>maga in modor,   þeah wæs hyre mægdenhad
>æghwæs onwalg.

First of all, there is a logical difficulty, since on logical grounds we should expect the *þeah*-member to be nondependent, 'and yet . . . .' This need not be treated too seriously however, since grammatical and logical expression are at variance elsewhere in unambiguous cases.[4] For instance:

>7 þær wearð þara Denescra micle ma ofslegenra. þeah ðe
>hie wælstowe geweald ahtan.   (ASC A 1001)

Here the group *þeah ðe* makes it certain that grammatically this member is dependent. Compare also ASC A 905; in ASC C 1041 the reverse occurs and a logically dependent *þeah*-member is grammatically nondependent; so too Rid 6/6. In the case of Chr 1418, however, there is a second difficulty; the word order of the *þeah*-member is not the regular one which, as we have seen above, obtains in two-thirds of the dependent members in the poetry.[5] The indicative in this example should also therefore be treated with reserve.

We are left with five unchallenged instances of the indicative in dependent *þeah*-members: Gen 733, Rid 95/10, Bo 29/49, Beo 1612, 2466, that is, 2.2 per cent of the total of the verbs in dependent *þeah*-members. This figure is a little higher than Burnham's for the prose; in the dozen texts on which she bases her analysis (p. 24), there are 10 cases of the indicative, 1.4 per cent of the total. Wilde's figure of 4 per cent ('Aufforderung' 356) for both verse and prose is unreliable, not because of his formal criteria but because his survey is not wide enough, revealing only 69 verbs, 3 of them indicative.

There is clearly a sharp and almost universally held distinction in mood between the verbs in dependent and nondependent *þeah*-members.[6] In one place we may even see this distinction being put into operation; the prose Boethius (136/28) has a nondependent *þeah*-member, 'þeah

---

4. Cf. Holthausen, *Altsächs. Element.* §542 Anm.
5. This order (cf. Andrew's 'demonstrative' order, *Syntax and Style* 1-2) is not very common in nondependent members either, as we saw in II.3; we can however compare 'Ðeah mæg sige' Wald II 25, 'þeah bið sum corn' Bo 22/37, 'þeah wæs magorinca mod' Bo 1/26.
6. Cf. Curme, *Syntax* 333.

habbað gemænlice,' which the versifier reorientates and makes a dependent member reading 'þeah ... hæbben' (Bo 29/90). Compare also Bo 24/46 'ðeah ðu hi nu geta ... hæbbe' which replaces a concessive-equivalent relative clause in the prose, 'þe ðu nu geot ... hafst.'

The relation of indicative to subjunctive in dependent members will be compared with other grammatical and logical features in II.14. Meantime we have seen enough to conclude that the indicative in these members is a very rare and sporadic feature and that those scholars who deny the inherently subjunctive character of dependent *þeah*-members are giving grossly undue prominence to the irregular.

8. PATTERN IN CONCESSIVE SENTENCES

Out of the considerable variety of concessive sentences formed with *þeah*, one pattern is clearly recurrent; it consists of a negative statement—usually strongly negative—followed by a positive dependent *þeah*-member. For example:

> No þæt þin aldor æfre wolde
> godes goldfatu in gylp beran,
> ne ðy hraðor hremde, ðeah ðe here brohte
> Israela gestreon in his æhte geweald   (Dan 753)

Further examples of this pattern are Gen 828, 952, 1037, Ex 140, 259, Dan 222, 695, ChrSat 515, And 561, 709, 954, 1215, 1609, El 81, 361, 477, 705, Prec 70, Rid 13/5, 18/1, 93/18, Leiden 13, Wald I 12. But it is characteristic above all of Beo:

> no ðy ær suna sinum syllan wolde,
> hwatum Heorowearde, þeah he him hold wære,
> breostgewædu.   (Beo 2160)
>
> no ymbe ða fæhðe spræc,
> þeah ðe he his broðor bearn abredwade.   (Beo 2618)

Compare also Beo 583, 679, 1096, 1612, 1659, 1940, 2217, 2466, 2855. On the further association of strong negative expression with concessive constructions, see below, III.12, IV.6, 12.

9. PARALLEL DEPENDENT MEMBERS

More than one dependent *þeah*-member may be in parallel concessive relation with the same nondependent member, and this is particularly common in the highly wrought periods of Bo. Thus:

>   Þeah him eall sie
> þes middangeard . . .
>
> þeah nu anra hwa   ealles wealde
> þæs iglandes . . .
>
> þeah he nu þæt eall   agan mote,
> hwy bið his anwald   auhte ðy mara   (Bo 16/8)

Parallel dependent members complete with finite verbs also occur with ellipsis of the subordinating conjunction in the second member, which usually takes the form of a variation of the first. For example:

> breat bolgenmod   beodgeneatas,
>   . . . oþ þæt he ana hwearf,
> mære þeoden   mondreamum from,
> ðeah þe hine mihtig God   mægenes wynnum,
> eafeþum stepte,   ofer ealle men
> forð gefremede.   (Beo 1713)

Similar instances of a single *þeah* (*þe*) governing more than one verb are to be found in Lord's Prayer II 104, Exhort 22, Bo 7/45, 10/27, 63, 13/18, 14/1, 29/51, ParPs 54/11, 131/3. There are no examples of *þe* being used with the second dependent member as a substitute conjunction in the way that *that* was to be used at a later stage of the language:

> *Though* yet of Hamlet our dear brother's death
> The memory be green, and *that* it us befitted
> To bear our hearts in grief . . .
> Yet so far hath discretion fought with nature . . .
>   (*Hamlet* I.ii.1)

10. CONCESSIVE PHRASES WITH *þeah*

Concessions of the type, 'We continued running, though tired' or '... and yet reluctantly,' are rare in OE. There is not a single dependent *þeah*-phrase in the poetry, and phrases in nondependent function occur only sporadically:

                        Saga ecne þonc
    mærum meotodes sunu   þæt ic his modor gewearð,
    fæmne forð seþeah   (Chr 209)

Compare also Bo 20/52, 229, Dan 513. The nondependent member in Sol 442 comes into this class obviously by ellipsis of the auxiliary verb in the previous line:

    and to his freondum wile   fultum secan,
    ðeh hwæðre godcundes   gæstes brucan.

11. ELLIPTICAL CONCESSIONS

Of sentences like 'He plays well, though his brother plays better,' Burnham says: "There is no real conflict of ideas here; the second clause enters as an afterthought, which has not sufficient importance to be given a new sentence" (p. 4, cf. also p. 33). Failure to recognize this type of sequence as concessive also mars R. A. Williams' argument in dealing with the crux in Beo 1129.[7] The phenomenon is mentioned somewhat facetiously by Eric Partridge[8] ('He, though a gentleman of property, was unhappily paralysed' *The Times* Feb. 1869) and by Lerch. The latter comments, "*Quoiqu'elle soit pauvre, elle est honnête* würde der pessimistischen Meinung Ausdruck geben, dass Armut normalerweise Unehrlichkeit mit sich bringt, was hier nur ausnahmsweise, auffälligerweise nicht der Fall sei ..."[9] But Behaghel's analysis of it as due to ellipsis has hardly been bettered. Sentences of this kind, he says,[1] arise through the agency of an intermediate thought or through an attempt to express linguistically a blend of two notions, as in Luther's 'Love ceases not, though prophecies do,'

---

7. *The Finn Episode in Beowulf* 88.
8. *Usage and Abusage* (London 1947) s.v. *though*.
9. *Hist. franz. Synt.* I.195.
1. *Deutsche Syntax* III.§1422.

CONCESSIONS FORMED WITH þeah II. 12

that is, 'though much ceases, for example prophecies.' Behaghel gives a good example from *Heliand* 229: 'thoh he ni mugi enig word sprecan, thoh mag he bi bocstabon bref gewirkean,' where we must supply the elliptical link '(yet he can) express himself in some ways.'

There are numerous examples of the phenomenon in OE. For instance:

> þær wearð ofslægen Lucumon . . . 7 Wulfheard . . . 7 ealra monna Fresiscra 7 Engliscra · lxii · 7 þara Deniscena · cxx · þa com þæm Deniscum scipum þeh ær flod to, ær þa Cristnan mehten hira ut ascufan, 7 hie forðy ut oðreowon
>
> (ASC A 897)

Behind this elliptical use of *þeh*, we see that the thought was something like, 'Although the Danes were having the worst of it, they were not annihilated because the tide enabled them to get away.' Compare in the poetry:

> Fyl nu þa frumspræce,   þeah þe user fea lifgen   (Az 42)
> *Ne bið fah wið me,
> þonne (..)unmægas   eft ongynnað,
> mecum gemetað,   swa ge me dydon.
> Ðeah mæg sige syllan   se ðe symle byð
> recon and rædfest   ryh(.)a gehwilces.
>   *MS: he   (Wald II 22)

Note also Gl 1163, DeathEdward 25, Gen 360, Dan 580.

12. *þeah* AS 'EVEN THOUGH'

The expression of that limit of concessive feeling which today we associate with 'even' was usual in OE without distinction[2] from ordinary concessive relations employing *þeah*. It is true that occasionally we have OE *efne* used for this purpose in nondependent members; Rune 51 says, 'the poplar bears no fruit; even so (*efne swa ðeah*), without seed, it brings forth suckers.' Compare also Hell 129, Rid 65/1, Bo 9/38. Occasionally too we find the particle *ge* (cf. BTS, s.v.) associated with 'even' concessions:

> Forþon þe wære selle   swiþe micle
> . . . . .

---

[2]. At least in words; there may have been a different intonation.

> þær þu wurde æt frumsceafte fugel   oþþe fisc on sæ,
> . . . . .
> ge þeah þu wære wyrmcynna   þæt wyrreste
>
> (Soul II 71)

Normally, however, we have simply *þeah* (*þe*) with the subjunctive exactly as for ordinary concessions. For example:

> Ðeah ge minne *flæschoman   fyres wylme
> forgripen gromhydge   gifran lege,
> næfre ge mec of þissum wordum onwendað   þendan mec min
>   gewit gelæsteð.   MS: flæs homan   (Gl 374)[3]

Other typical examples are Gen 828, Jul 494, 515, Gl 240, 273, 299, 377, 466, Rid 40/46, 64, ParPs 54/11, 137/7, Bo 14/1 (2x), 22/43, Beo 1368.

13. CONDITIONAL AND OTHER NONCONCESSIVE USES OF *þeah*

Bøgholm (*The Layamon Texts* 60) finds that *þeah* and *gif* are to some extent interchangeable in the Layamon manuscripts in both conditional and concessive function, just as today *though* is conditional in *as though* and *if* is concessive in *even if*. Burnham finds similar examples of conditional *þeah* in OE prose (p. 35), although the only example quoted is the following, from Liebermann's edition of the Laws (Halle 1903, p. 360): 'þonne andwyrdan þa yrfenuman swa he sylf sceolde þeah he lif hæfde.'[1]

In OE poetry however there is not a single example of *þeah* that can be said with certainty to be deliberately conditional. It is true that in ParPs 131/3 the OE, corresponding to two Latin conditional clauses followed by a temporal one ('si . . . si . . . donec . . .'), has '*þeah þe* . . . *gif* . . . *oþþæt*'; but while the *þeah þe* clause has to be translated as conditional, it seems likely that the translator misunderstood the first *si*, thinking it meant 'even though'; there is an example of *þeah þe* translating such a concessive *si* in ParPs 61/11, and failure to understand the Latin text is not uncommon in ParPs (cf. 59/3, 73/19). In addition, there is Bo 13/18 where a dependent *þeah*-member has also been occasionally interpreted as conditional; here,

---

3. Cf. in prose usage: '7 þeah man asette twegen fætels full ealað oððe wæteres, hy gedoð þæt oþer bið oferfroren, sam hit sy sumor sam winter' Oros 21/15 (Sweet emends *oþer* to *ægþer*).

4. Cf. also Williams, *The Finn Episode* 88f.

however, the text is obviously confused and the *þeah*-member plainly corresponds to a normal concessive use of *þeah* in the prose. The conditional function of *þeah* must therefore be said to be extremely rare in OE and probably not in evidence at all in the poetry.

Nonconcessive uses of *þeah* in the poetry seem in fact to be mainly due to failure in logical arrangement or to confusion or weakness of construction. In Chr 1305, for instance, we find *swa þeah* acting as little more than a neutral connective:

> Ne mæg þurh þæt flæsc se scrift
> geseon on þære sawle, hwæþer him mon soð þe lyge
> sagað on hine sylfne, þonne he þa synne bigæð.
> Mæg mon swa þeah gelacnigan leahtra gehwylcne,
> yfel unclæne

Compare also Dan 237, Hell 118.

Cobb [5] accepts the following *þeah* construction as concessive, with 'subjunctive of ideal possibility':

> Nat þeah þu mid ligenum fare
> þurh dyrne geþanc þe þu drihtnes eart
> boda of heofnum. (Gen 531)

This is scarcely tenable however and we should, with Klaeber [6] and B. J. Timmer,[7] interpret *þeah . . . þe* as 'whether . . . or'; for *nytan þeah* thus used in OE prose, see Burnham p. 34, and for *þe* in various expressions meaning 'whether . . . or,' see BT s.v. *þe*.

For the sake of completeness, I now list all the poetic examples of *þeah* used weakly or plainly without concessive feeling: Gen 531, Dan 237, Jul 490, ParPs 72/11, 131/3, Bo 13/18, Beo 1129, 2217, Chr 1305, Hell 118. This list covers *þeah* in both dependent and nondependent members.

14. INQUIRY INTO THE RELATION BETWEEN VARIOUS FACTORS

1. Incidence of *þeah–þeah þe* to correlation: there seems to be no relation between these factors, except possibly in the case of correlations using *hwæðere*, where six have *þeah þe* and only one has *þeah*.

---

5. 'Subjunctive Mood' 53f.
6. *The Later Genesis* (Heidelberg 1913) 51.
7. *The Later Genesis* 26, 108, 130.

2. Incidence of *þeah–þeah þe* to a particular order of dependent and nondependent members: there seems to be no relation; for example, the four texts which have the largest number of initially placed dependent members (Gl, Ph, Bo, and ParPs) differ considerably in their choice of subordinating conjunctions.

3. Incidence of *þeah–þeah þe* to a particular word order: there is no evidence of any relation; for instance, Gen and Bo agree in using *þeah* predominantly, but while Gen keeps to the 'regular' word order, Bo departs from it more than any other text.

4. Incidence of *þeah–þeah þe* to the meaning 'even though': for every instance of *þeah þe* meaning 'even though,' there are two instances of *þeah*, and this is too near the general proportion of *þeah þe* to *þeah* for us to suspect a special relation.

5. Incidence of *þeah–þeah þe* to the use of the indicative: the five dependent members containing unquestionable instances of the indicative are all introduced by *þeah*, but it would be unwise to base any conclusion on such slight material, especially as the almost certain case of the indicative in Husband 35 has *þeah þe*, and, if the common emendation is correct, this is true also of Soul 1 135.

6. Incidence of *indicative–subjunctive* to the 'reality' of concessions: it has long been accepted that a relation exists between these factors,[8] but the evidence for making a positive claim is very slender. At any rate, it is beyond dispute that the subjunctive is used throughout OE for 'real' concessions as well as 'unreal'; the only point in doubt is whether the 'reality' of those concessions expressed with the indicative is significant. The five safe instances of the indicative in dependent members are all operating 'real' concessions and this is true also of the three other possible examples. But beyond stating that there is no evidence of the indicative being used for 'unreal' concessions there is little that we can say. In Beo 202 we read, 'Men did not blame him for going, *though he was dear to them*'; in 2160, 'He would not give them to his son, *though he was loyal to him*'; in 2466, 'He could not persecute the warrior, *though he was hateful to him*.' In the first two cases we have the subjunctive, in the third the indicative; he would be bold who asserted that this indicative deliberately matched the 'reality' of the concession.

---

8. See Delbrück, PBBeit xxix.301 and Horn, 'Untersuchungen' 215; cf. Behre, *Subjunctive in Old English Poetry* 122–3 and Wilde, 'Aufforderung' 357–9.

15. LATIN ORIGINALS AND PARALLEL VERSIONS

The poetry furnishes a good deal of material to be compared profitably with other versions. First, there are some items of verse existing in two OE poetical versions; Rid 35 is a WS parallel to the Nb text, Leiden, and it is worth noting that they agree (*hwæþre seþeah, huethrae suae ðeh*), despite the vagaries of copyists, in the rendering of Aldhelm's 'et tamen.' It is also of interest to compare Dan 325 with Az 42; both have dependent members with subjunctive verbs, but while they agree in putting these dependent members in final position, they disagree in the form of the conjunction: Dan has *ðeah*, Az *þeah þe*.

Secondly, we have the verse rendering of the Boethian *Metres* which, it is generally agreed, was based on the OE prose translation of the Latin.[9] A good many of the *þeah*-concessions in the verse correspond closely in expression to those in the prose, for example, 20/136, 142, 31/10 (nondependent members), 2/4, 10/7, 63, 13/35 (dependent members). Much more rarely the poetic version reduces the formal strength of the concessive expression. This is done once in the case of a nondependent *þeah*-member (30/5) which corresponds to an elaborate correlation in the prose employing *þeah* three times, and twice in the case of dependent members (10/24, 26) where the verse reduces the correlative forms of the prose. But most of the concessions in the verse either have a more enhanced form than the corresponding prose ones or are absent from the prose entirely:

Nondependent members:

9/34	swa þeah	Prose:	þeah
11/43	and swa þeah	"	7 þeah
15/7	swa þeah . . . þeah . . .	"	þeah . . . ac . . .
19/5	swa ðeah	"	þeah
20/52	hwæðre þeah . . . swa ðeah	"	þeah
20/164	þeah . . . þeah	"	þeah
20/229	na hwæðre þeah	"	7 þeah
23/1	ðeah gita	"	get
20/157	and þeah	"	7
10/14	and . . . þeah	"	concession not explicit
2/8	and þeah	"	no concession
7/14	and þeah	"	" "
13/6	and þeah	"	" "
1/25	þeah	"	" "
26/95	þeah	"	" "

9. See ASPR v.xlvff. for a discussion of this point, with references.

Dependent members:

16/8	þeah . . . þeah . . . þeah . . . (parallel)	Prose:	þeah . . . þeah . . . (parallel)
7/45	þeah . . . þeah þe . . . (parallel)	"	þeah
20/63	þeah . . . þeah . . . (correlative)	"	þeah
24/44	þeah ðu hi nu geta forgiten hæbbe	"	þe ðu nu geot forgiten hafst
7/34	þeah	"	no concession
15/13	Ðeah	"	" "
18/5	þeah	"	" "
20/114	þeah	"	" "
22/43	þeah	"	" "
25/69	ðeah	"	" "
29/49	þeah	"	" "
30/9	þeah	"	" "

There is some evidence that in the verse the initial placing of dependent members is influenced by the usage in the prose. In four instances where the dependent member does not appear in the prose (7/34, 22/43, 25/69, 29/49), it takes up final position; nevertheless, we cannot be certain that the versifier's natural tendency is to conform to normal usage, since on another occasion (15/13) he puts initially one of the dependent members which he introduces himself, and two more (18/5, 30/9) he places medially.

Lastly, we come to the poems which are based, more or less closely, on Latin originals. In only three cases (each in ParPs) do we find a reasonably balanced correspondence between the Latin and English expressions: 'Divitiæ si affluant' is rendered (61/11) by 'Þeah þe eow wealan to . . . flowen'; *etsi* (54/11) and *si* (137/7) by *þeah þe*. In 77/20, 'Ac . . . þeah þe . . . hwæðere' is a reorientation of the Latin 'Numquid . . .? Quoniam . . . Numquid' (cf. VespPs: 'ah . . . forðon . . . ah . . .'). Twice at least the OE translator has a *þeah* construction because he misunderstands the Latin: 73/19, 131/3, in the second case rendering conditional *si* by *þeah þe* (see above, II.13). In half a dozen cases (all in ParPs), the translator either makes more explicit or exaggerates the form of the concessive expression; thus:

68/31	þeah þe him upp aga horn . . .	Latin:	cornua producentem
88/31	ac . . . swa þeah	"	autem

89/10	þeah þe	"	autem (but without exact correspondence)
113/16	þeah þe hi ceolan habban	"	Non clamabunt in gutture suo (zero relating element)
118/157	swa þeah hwæðere	"	zero relating element

There are no fewer than eleven *þeah*-concessions in ParPs and Rid 40 (based on Aldhelm's *De Creatura*) which are not matched by concessions of any sort in the Latin: ParPs 72/11, 77/63, 108/1, 128/5 (2x), 134/17, 138/13, 146/11, Rid 40/27, 46, 64.

Two important features stand out as a result of this survey: first, that a large number of the most formal concessive expressions in OE poetry are introduced without warrant from OE prose or Latin originals; secondly, that it is a characteristic of the poetry to increase the formal strength of concessive expressions taken from originals. These both suggest that it is wrong to assume that OE writers tended naturally to use a 'primitive' syntax with predominantly paratactic expressions of notional relationship, and indulged in more formal or hypotactic expressions only in *direct* imitation of Latin.

III

Nondependent Concessions Without *þeah*

1. *hwæðere*

NEXT to *þeah*, *hwæðere* is the most essentially concessive element in OE. This is not to say that second only to *þeah*, *hwæðere* is used to form most of the OE concessions; indeed, only 83 concessions in the poetry use *hwæðere* without an accompanying *þeah*; but it is a word which is confined to the concessive function to a degree only comparable with *þeah*.

We have already seen (II.2) that *hwæðere* is used a number of times as a reinforcing or correlating element in conjunction with *þeah*. In nondependent concessions without *þeah*, *hwæðere* is distributed as follows : Gen 6 times (none in Gen B), Dan 3, And 2, Rood 6, El 1, Chr 3, Gl 4, Ph 3, Gift 1, Wid 1, Soul II 1, Wulf 1, Rid 8, Resig 2, ParPs 18, Bo 5, Sol 3, Menol 1, Psalm 50 1, Ruthwell 1, Beo 12. A typical example is Ph 364:

                      Þonne him weorþeð
ende lifes;   hine ad þeceð
þurh æledfyr.   Hwæþre eft cymeð
aweaht wrætlice   wundrum to life.

The situation seems to be very different in the prose. Burnham (pp. 17f.) gives one or two rather dubious examples of *hwæðere* as a subordinating conjunction (there is no trace of such a function in the verse) and on pp. 67f. a few examples of relative clauses having concessive force in which (*þonne*) *hwæðere*, as she points out, is " a direct translation " of Latin relative clauses containing *tamen*. Moreover, in ParPs, *hwæðere* (which often translates *verumtamen*) usually corresponds to the reinforced group *ah hweðre* in VespPs (for example, 61/5, 72/14), and not to the simple *hweðre*. Bo is also illuminating in this respect; its 150 concessions, often based firmly on the prose original, include only five formed with *hwæðere* alone, and none of these takes its form from the prose. It is not true however that the common poetic function of *hwæðere* is unknown in original OE prose; thus we find: '7 se casere ahte wælstowe geweald. 7 hwæðere he þær wæs miclum geswenced. ær he þanon hwurfe' (ASC C 982). See further BT, BTS, s.v. But standing alone, it is relatively rarer in the prose of OE than in the verse. Even in the poetry itself there seem to be considerable restrictions on its use; it is fairly rare in the Cynewulfian poems and absent from Gen B.[1]

As with other concessive constructions, the concessive relationship signaled by *hwæðere* is sometimes notionally elliptical. Thus:

    Hycge him halig folc   hælu to drihtne;
    doð eowre heortan hige   hale and clæne,
    forðon eow god standeð   georne on fultum.
    Hwæðere ge, manna bearn,   manes unlyt
    wyrceað on wægum   (ParPs 61/8)

Sometimes too, the concessive relation is very weak, with *hwæðere* corresponding to the frequent use of 'however' in NE as an almost neutral connective:

        þæs wraðe ongeald
  hearde mid hiwum   hægstealdra wyn.
  Ongæt hwæðere   gumena aldor
  hwæt him waldend wræc   witeswingum;
  heht him Abraham to   (Gen 1861)

'Pharaoh received vicious punishment; however, he was not long realizing the cause.' Compare also Dan 549, Chr 449, Rood 55 (Ruthwell 10).

This phenomenon shades off imperceptibly, as is particularly noticeable in Rood, into the purely nonconcessive function of *hwæðere*. In Rood, *hwæðere* occurs six times certainly or almost certainly in concessive function, but it occurs three times with no concessive feeling at all; for example:

        Geseah ic þæt fuse beacen
  wendan wædum ond bleom;   hwilum hit wæs mid wætan
        bestemed,
  beswyled mid swates gange,   hwilum mid since gegyrwed.
    Hwæðre ic þær licgende   lange hwile
  beheold hreowcearig   hælendes treow,
  oððæt ic gehyrde   þæt hit hleoðrode.   (21)

Dickins and Ross[2] distinguish this use of *hwæðere* (glossed as 'and')

---

[1]. It is also absent from the *Heliand*. In English however, as the NED shows, it was used to point concessions as late as the 15th century, at least in northern dialects.

[2]. *Dream of the Rood*, Glossary, s.v. Cf. also Sievers, PBBeit ix.138, Klaeber, AngliaBeib xvii.102.

from the more usual concessive one. The other cases of nonconcessive *hwæðere* are Rood 59, 67; in ParPs 136/8 *hwæðere* seems to be an error for the pronoun *hwæðer*.

The great majority of *hwæðere*-members contain a finite verb, but occasionally the verb is omitted in an elliptical expression:

Wangas ymbelicgað,
eorðe ælgreno,   eac hwæðre ceald.   (Bo 20/75)

So too, ParPs 72/18. As to the mood in *hwæðere*-members, since they are notionally the apodoses of the concessions to which they belong, we neither expect nor find subjunctive verbs, unless of course (as in ParPs 88/42) the subjunctive is required for some reason other than the concession.

It is clearly normal for *hwæðere* to take initial position in its member, and this obtains in about two-thirds of the examples; *hwæðere* begins its member (which is sometimes linked to the preceding member by *and*) 53 times; in another 5 cases it is only preceded by the strong negative form *no*; in 25 cases it is placed later in the member. The details are as follows:

hwæðere–subject–object/complement–verb:

Gen 2362, Dan 549, Rood 37, Gl 440, Rid 31/6, Resig 67, ParPs 61/4, 8, 67/20, 68/3, 72/13, 88/42, 90/7, 118/22, 67, Bo 20/75 (verb and subject zero), Psalm 50/6, Beo 553, 572, 575, 887, 967, 2226 (?—MS defective), 2296, 2377.
Total: 25.

hwæðere–subject–verb (–object/complement):

Gen 1857, And 1481, Rood 14, 55 (Ruthwell 10), 101, El 716, Chr 449, Gl 231, Ph 364, Rid 39/18, ParPs 84/7, 87/15, Beo 1269.
Total: 14.

hwæðere (–object/complement)–verb–subject:

Gen 212, Dan 546, And 501, Chr 706, 1376, Gl 552, Ph 219, Rid 31/16, Sol 175, 437, Beo 1713, 2096.
Total: 12.

hwæðere–object/complement–subject–verb:

Rood 75, Beo 2873.
Total: 2.

no hwæðere, with subject, object, etc. preceding verb in various orders:

Gen 1455, 1724, Dan 163, Wid 35, Rid 31/6.
Total: 5.

verb (–subject)–hwæðere–etc.:

Rood 42, Gift 30, Soul II 39, Wulf 11, Rid 3/53, 22/10, 54/7, ParPs 113/13, Bo 20/150, 168, 26/98, Sol 328, Menol 68.
Total: 13.

verb–hwæðere–subject–etc.:

Gen 1861, Ph 437.
Total: 2.

subject–hwæðere–verb–etc.:

Gl 517, ParPs 58/5, 113/15, 134/18.
Total: 4.

verb (–etc.) preceding hwæðere:

Rid 58/2, Resig 25, ParPs 72/18 (verb elliptical), 118/141, 139/12, Bo 20/72.
Total: 6.

No account is given of the position of nonconcessive *hwæðere*, but it does not present any significantly different pattern.

The consideration of Latin and other OE versions provides some interesting points. In Rood 55 we find the Vercelli Book in agreement with the Ruthwell Cross in the use of *hwæðere* and in the position of the adversative:

> Krist wæs on rodi.
> Hweþræ þer fusæ fêarran kwomu
> æþþilæ til anum.   (10)

In Bo, none of the five instances of concessive *hwæðere* is taken from the prose original; the prose version indeed makes no use of this element. Twice it replaces *þeah* in the prose (Bo 20/152,[3] 26/100); for the rest, the particular concessive relations are absent from the prose (20/74, 78, 170).

In ParPs, *hwæðere* translates *verumtamen* seven times: 61/4, 8, 67/20, 72/13, 84/7, 90/7, 139/12; but although *verumtamen* is normally placed initially, the translator does not necessarily follow the word order of his original: 'Verumtamen justi' is rendered 'Soð is hwæðere,' 139/12. Twice *hwæðere* corresponds to *autem* (87/15, 118/23), though once with a shift of emphasis, and *hwæðere* once translates *propterea* (118/67) which is used concessively in the Latin. Once the translator gives a concessive twist not apparent in the Latin:

---

3. In this case, perhaps, because *hwæðre* conveniently takes the alliteration in the second half-line.

'hwæðere ic . . . gewene' for 'Dum spero' (68/3); cf. VespPs, 'ðonne ic gehyhtu.' Twice *hwæðere* has nothing to correspond in the Latin (58/5, 118/141), and once (136/8, probably in error for *hwæðer*) it corresponds to *qui*. For the rest, we find *hwæðere*, preceded by *and* or *ne*, making more explicit the relation conveyed in the Latin solely by the adversative use of *et*: 72/18, 88/42, 113/13, 15, 134/18.

We may sum up our findings in this section as follows. The element *hwæðere*, when not used in conjunction with *þeah*, is almost entirely confined to concessive use in OE, though this use seems commoner in poetry than in prose; *hwæðere* usually takes initial position in its member but in about one-third of the cases it takes up medial or even final position, and when not initial it is nearly always preceded by its accompanying verb. It corresponds to the Latin *verumtamen* or else is used to make a concession more explicit than in the Latin.

2. *ac*

Unlike *hwæðere*, the concessive function of *ac* seems commoner in prose than in verse; although the ASC, for example, is not nearly so extensive as the combined poetic texts nor contains nearly so many examples of concession, it presents more than 100 examples of concessive *ac*, while the entire corpus of poetry has only 44. Indeed, *ac* may well be the leading sign of concession in the prose: the 'Ohthere and Wulfstan' portion of Oros has 14 concessions, 6 of them formed with *ac*; ASC has nearly 400 concessions, over 100 of them formed with *ac*. In these prose texts, it may also be pointed out that *ac* is used a further five times to reinforce *þeah*-concessions while in the poetry *ac* reinforces *þeah* only once. Similarly, while *ac* itself is not reinforced in the verse, several reinforcements are found in OE prose; thus, 'ac . . . gyt' ASC E 1009, 'ac for eallum þissum' E 1006.

The impression that *ac* plays a leading part in prose concessions is not confirmed by Burnham, who devotes no section to this connective and mentions only incidentally (for example, pp. 104f.) constructions formed with it. This could be for one of two reasons. The leadership of *ac* in ASC might well not be general throughout the body of OE prose; Burnham seems to pay little attention to ASC, concentrating more on the homilies and on translations from Latin. This reason has little basis however; one cannot go far in reading Ælfric (to whom Burnham pays particular attention) without coming upon concessions formed with *ac*, and the Ælfredian Bede seems to have them even more frequently. The second possibility, and this seems more likely, is that, under the influence of contemporary grammars which stress the importance of *though* in NE concessions and neglect or ignore *but*, Burnham was concerned with analyzing dependent to the exclusion of nondependent concessions.

The distribution of concessive *ac* in OE poetry is as follows: Gen 5 (4 in Gen B), Ex 1, ChrSat 4, And 1, El 1, Chr 2, Rid 3, ParPs 2, Bo 12, Finn 1, ASC Poems 1, Jud II 2, Lord's Prayer II 1, Prayer 1, Fasting 2, Beo 4, Jud 1. Members introduced by *ac*, being notionally apodoses, have no influence exerted on the mood of their verbs by the concessive relation. The following is a typical example of *ac* in concessive function:

> Ðonne firena bearn
> tearum geotað, þonne þæs tid ne biþ,
> synne cwiþað; ac hy to sið doð
> gæstum helpe (Chr 1565)

Verbless *ac*-members are exceptional:

> He mid lyt wordum ac geleaffullum
> his hæle begeat (Jud II 61)

As regards word order, concessions with *ac* demonstrate even greater regularity than do those with *hwæðere*; in the overwhelming majority of cases the order is *ac–subject–verb–etc.* Very occasionally, inversion of subject and verb is found; for example, 'Ac arisan ongan rices ealdor' Fasting 31; cf. also Beo 1659, Jud 181. Occasionally too, the verb goes into final position: 'ac ic þine bebodu efnde and læste' ParPs 118/143.

Elliptical concessions like the following seem frequent with *ac*:

> ... hwi swigast þu, synnigu tunge,
> . . . . .
> ne þe ælmihtig . . .
> heofonrices weard, gehyreð mid lustum?
> Ac se dæg cymeð ðonne demeð god
> eorðan ymbhwyrft (Jud II 67)

Here the underlying concession, 'Although you can now approach a sympathetic God, the day comes when he will be your judge,' is not actually expressed. Compare in OE prose:

> Þa *Beormas hæfdon swiþe wel gebud hira land; ac hie ne dorston þær on cuman. *MS: First stroke of *m* erased.
> (Oros 17/27)

The real concession intended here seems to be, 'Although they would have liked to see the B.s' land, because it was well cultivated, they did not dare to investigate.'

One type of disjunctive ellipsis is noteworthy. For example:

> Eala, þær hit wurde oððe wolde god
> þæt on eorðan nu ussa tida
> geond þas widan weoruld wæren æghwæs
> swelce under sunnan. Ac hit is sæmre nu (Bo 8/39)

Other examples are Bo 17/16, 21/18, ChrSat 109,[4] and probably Finn 8. A similar but probably nonconcessive use of *ac* is to be found in Gen 368, 386.

Unlike *hwæðere, ac* is by no means restricted to the concessive function with a mere handful of exceptions. The elliptical use of *ac* at times becomes very hard to distinguish from its nonconcessive uses, and one of the greatest difficulties encountered in the functional analysis of OE concessions is to discern the meaning of *ac* in individual contexts. Thus while the figures given relate to what seem to be definite examples of concession, there are besides many examples of *ac* used in a nonconcessive but perhaps closely related function. Indeed, there are no less than 30 such dubious cases in the verse.

Fifteen of these are in Sol where *ac* is used in an interesting function very common with *but* today. While *but* is the chief concessive element in modern colloquial English, it is used for many other idiomatic purposes; one is what we may call the 'subject-changing' function:[5]

> . . . it cannot be much longer before God calls me to your side. But I forget my duties. (Alison's Island)
> It's a satisfying place, a contenting sort of a place. But I see the cards are dealt. (Ibid.)

In the dialogue between Solomon and Saturn, *ac* is frequently used to change the subject in this way at the beginning of each fresh question. For example:

> Saturnus cuæð:
> " Ac hwæt is se dumba . . . (Sol 230)
> Saturnus cwæð:
> " Ac hwa demeð . . . (Sol 336)

It might be argued that this *ac* is elliptically concessive, since in the cases quoted Saturn's question follows a satisfactory answer by Solomon to a previous question, *ac* thus signifying, 'All right, even though you have managed that, what about this—who, etc.' But this

---

4. Cf. Meroney, JEGPh xli.201ff.
5. Cf. Wendt, *Syntax* 246, on the 'überleitend' function of *but*.

obviously does not hold for some of the examples, where the previous speaker has only asked a question and done no answering at all, as in 340, 344. The only function that can be common to all these parallel examples of *ac* is the non-concessive ' subject-changing ' one.

But it is the adversative use of *ac* which is most difficult to separate from the concessive use. Many grammarians have tried to establish the exact frontier between these two relationships, but in studying written language the last resort (and this is all too frequently reached) must be to rely on subjective judgment. Schücking's analysis of Beo 1131 shows us what his criteria are, despite his confusion of the adversative relation with elliptical concession. How, he asks, could the impossibility of Hengest's going home stop him from thinking about it?[6] The distinction implied in this question has appeared the most essential to many grammarians. The adversative particle becomes concessive, says Dubislav, as soon as the content of the clause so introduced appears to depend on that of the main clause.[7] Ohlander simplifies the distinction by making the degree of unexpectedness in the relationship the essential criterion,[8] and Eugen Lerch, who has perhaps given more thought to this question than any other grammarian, seems to establish the soundness of this analysis beyond reasonable doubt. In the concessive relation, he says, " Der Gegensatz ist nach Meinung des Sprechenden so stark, dass die beiden Tatsachen sich eigentlich ausschliessen müssten: eine erwartete ursächliche Folge bleibt aus, ihr Gegenteil tritt ein."[9]

Nevertheless, in dealing with what has been prettily called such " a will o' the wisp," " an essence so ethereal " as concession,[1] we must expect differences of approach to continue to appear. Brunot, for instance, thinks that the speaker's attitude to the *truth* of what is said makes all the difference: " Il est souvent assez délicat de distinguer les oppositions de ces concessions. Considérons la phrase: *Sans être artiste, André goûtait les belles choses*...... Ce peut être une simple opposition. Mais mettez cette phrase dans une discussion. Supposez que ce soit la mère d'André qui la prononce, pour défendre son fils. Le *sans être artiste* manquera de conviction. C'est chose qu'elle veut bien reconnaître, mais elle ne l'affirme pas vraiment, on est en présence d'une concession."[2]

Indeed, especially in dealing with the written word alone, Lerch's parenthetic " nach Meinung des Sprechenden " quoted above and Horn's remark that " Der Gegensatz steckt nicht in den Worten, sondern in

---

6. *Die Grundzüge der Satzverknüpfung* §15.
7. 'Studien zur mittelenglischen Syntax' 304.
8. *Coordinate Expressions* 14, 34.
9. *Hist.franz.Synt.* 1, footnote to p. 359; cf. also 195ff., 263f., 266f., II.333.
1. Shearin, MLN xxvi.255.
2. *La Pensée et la langue* 855.

der Sache "³ suggest that a certain subjectivity is inevitable. The part played by the background and the speaker's attitude is shown by the following example. If the House of Lords is presumed to have a natural antipathy to the House of Commons, then Poutsma's illustration of the adversative relation is a sound one: " The Commons passed the Bill, but the Lords threw it out." ⁴ But if the Lords were regarded as sycophants who regularly took their cue from the Commons, the same statement becomes concessive, any difference being expressed by some such factor as intonation which leaves no mark on the written word. " Contrast easily becomes concession . . . Then the intonation —usually emphasized—is the sole bearer of the concessive idea." ⁵

In dealing with the borderline examples of *ac*, therefore, we must depend on context or on a verb of expectation or volition to show the writer's attitude to the content of the *ac*-member, and those examples have been excluded from the list of concessions in which the attitude was not quite clear, even though the writer may well have intended a concessive relation. It is preferable to have a smaller list of unquestionable concessions than to risk including nonconcessive examples.

In OE poetry, however, most of the examples of *ac* are neither concessive nor adversative, but correspond to *sondern* or to Swedish *men i stallet*. This function, in NE performed by *but*, is known variously as ' explanatory ' (Ohlander), ' annulling ' (*aufhebende*, Schücking), ' antithetic expansion ' (Williams), ' enhancing ' (Wendt), ' substitutive ' (Poutsma). For example, ' Remember, it wasn't Jenny Cranleigh who treated him like that, but little Jenny Heycroft long ago ' (Jenny).

The substitutive use of *ac*, being more remote notionally than the adversative from the concessive function, is usually easy to distinguish and requires no comment. For example:

> Synna ne cuþon,
> firena fremman,   ac hie on friðe lifdon,
> ece mid heora aldor.   (Gen 18)

But occasionally the text is sufficiently difficult as to cause differences of interpretation:

> Ne magon we þa tide   be getale healdan
> dagena rimes,   ne drihtnes stige
> on heofenas up,   forþan *þe hwearfað aa
> wisra gewyrdum,   ac sceal wintrum frod
> on circule cræfte findan
> halige dagas.   *MS: he   (Menol 63)

---

3. ' Untersuchungen ' 217.
4. *Late Modern English* 1.590.
5. M. Schubiger, *Role of Intonation* 29.

NONDEPENDENT CONCESSIONS WITHOUT þeah III.2

ASPR VI.171 shows that Professor Dobbie regards *ac* as concessive ("But a man wise in years will skilfully find . . ."), but it seems more likely to be substitutive, the general sense being, "We cannot determine the dates but rather it takes (*sceal* 'must') a scholar."

> Ne mostun hy Guðlaces   gæste sceþþan,
> ne þurh sarslege   sawle gedælan
> wið lichoman,   ac hy ligesearwum
> ahofun hearmstafas,   hleahtor alegdon,
> sorge seofedon,   þa hi swiðra oferstag
> weard on wonge.   (Gl 226)

Kennedy (*Poems of Cynewulf* 269) renders *ac* as 'yet' and Gollancz (*Exeter Book* 119) shows that his interpretation is similar, but, although *ligesearwum* makes it seem that the spirits took effective offensive action, the rest of the sentence seems to make it clear that *ac* here too is substitutive.

On the other hand, one cannot go all the way with Williams in his attempt to show that *ac* in *Beowulf* is always the "external sign of antithetic expansion" (*Finn Episode* 150). It is not enough to point to the pattern regularly found with substitutive *ac* (a negative statement followed by *ac*) and then claim that all cases of *ac* in this pattern are substitutive. True, it is fairly rare to find concessive or adversative *ac* in these circumstances, but sufficient examples occur to show that it is by no means impossible:

> Ne hafað hio sawle ne feorh,   ac hio siþas sceal
> geond þas wundorworuld   wide dreogan.   (Rid 39/16)

Here we can be quite certain that the relation is concessive, not merely from the content of the two lines, but from the fact that they are followed by a variation on the relationship in which *hwæþre* is used to signal the concession. Other examples are Rid 83/8, Ex 240, Chr 94. And of course in NE, concessive *but* is common after a preceding negative nondependent member: 'You won't be a great success, but your pretty face will ensure that you are never out of work' (Jenny). Nevertheless, Williams claims that in examples like the following *ac* is not concessive but means 'accordingly':

>   . . . he lust wigeð,
>   . . . secce ne weneþ
> to Gar-Denum.   Ac ic him Geata sceal
> eafoð ond ellen . . .
> guþe gebeodan.   (Beo 599)

Although the distinction between *Geata* and *Gar-Denum* might be felt to support a substitutive interpretation of *ac, weneþ* and the general context appear to make a concessive relation more likely; one may similarly disagree with Williams' interpretation of Beo 691, 1659, 2672 and consider that he has not proved his case against Schücking.[6]

There are not many opportunities in our material to trace *ac* back to a Latin model; the two concessive uses of *ac* in ParPs correspond to *sed* and *autem* (113/24, 118/143) respectively. It may be noted that in ASC a 443, *ac* corresponds to Bede's *tamen* (Plummer 1.28). The study of Bo in relation to the prose source is important in view of what has been said earlier about concessive *ac* belonging more to OE prose than to the poetry. No verse text has nearly such a high proportion of examples of concessive *ac* as Bo, and it is interesting to find that 10 out of the 12 cases correspond to *ac* in the prose and this apparently explains their place in the verse; the references are 5/21, 6/8, 8/39, 17/16, 19/24, 20/218, 21/18, 27/21, 28/64, 72. The two remaining examples are original concessions in the poetic version with nothing to correspond in the prose: 10/54, 28/35.

Thus, in summing up this section we can say that *ac* is used concessively considerably more in prose than in verse, and that the word order within the *ac*-member is usually *ac–subject–verb–etc.*; a few verbless members occur. Elliptical concessions with this construction are frequent and so are the nonconcessive (adversative and substitutive) functions of *ac*; indeed, the substitutive is more frequent than the concessive function in OE poetry. Frequently the adversative and occasionally the substitutive functions are difficult to distinguish from the concessive. The consideration of sources and parallel versions shows *ac* corresponding to Latin and OE prose nondependent constructions.

3. *and*

Although the copulative conjunction is often regarded as invariably 'neutral,' in many languages past and present it has a widespread adversative function. It may be pointed out that *and* is cognate with Latin *ante* and Greek *anti*. The concessive use of *und* in MHG has been noted by Behaghel and Sehrt,[7] in NHG by Wilmanns[8] amongst others; and the similar function of *and* in all periods of English has not altogether escaped notice.

6. *Satzverknüpfung* §50.
7. *Deutsche Syntax* III.§1424, and *Zur Geschichte der wg Konjunktion und* (Göttingen 1916) respectively.
8. *Deutsche Grammatik* III.I.260.

Considering that 4 per cent of the concessions in OE poetry are formed with *and* without other adversative, it is surprising that Burnham finds " the use of *and* to introduce a virtual concession " a " rare occurrence " (p. 95). Einenkel, while barely illustrating adversative *and* in OE,[9] does not even mention its concessive use. Even Maisenhelder's study of *Die altenglische Partikel* " *and*," which adequately demonstrates the causal and conditional functions (pp. 72, 78 respectively) and discusses the adversative function (pp. 69–70), makes no attempt to distinguish a concessive function. Ohlander's study of *Coordinate Expressions*, however, clearly shows that *and* is frequently used for concession in ME, and scholars like Wendt and Curme have analyzed its concessive functions today.[1]

Indeed, for the ME and NE periods it is difficult to see how one could avoid taking account of concessive *and*, since it occurs in some of the most striking passages in English literature. For example:

    Þou cowþez neuer God nauþer plese ne pray,
    Ne neuer nawþer Pater ne Crede;
    And quen mad on þe fyrst(e) day!   (*Pearl* 486)
    Allas! What sholden straunge to me doon,
    When he, that for my beste freend I wende,
    Ret me to love, and sholde it me defende?   (*Troilus* ii.411)
    . . . and 'tis believed by all
    That many and many a day he thither went,
    And never lifted up a single stone.   (*Michael* 466)

It is fairly common in good colloquial English of today (though not as frequent as the *but*-concession) as can be seen in the middle-class dialogue of the postwar plays: ' You've given me years of unhappiness, and ruined what might have been the loveliest part of my life—and you say you haven't done me any harm ' (Jenny).

Some of the OE examples justify Burnham's condemnation of the construction as " careless or illiterate " (p. 96), but many might well have earned Curme's comment: " coördination is much more expressive when there is feeling to be conveyed: ' Three thousand years *and* the world so little changed!' (Thoreau, *Journal*, 1, p. 31); more expressive than hypotactic: ' Although three thousand years have passed since Homer's times, the world has changed very little.' "[2]

In the corpus of OE poetry there are 60 unquestionable *and*-concessions, distributed as follows: Gen 2 (both in Gen B), Dan 2, ChrSat 2, And 4, Soul 1 1, HomFrag 1 3, Rood 1, El 4, Chr 5, Gl 3,

---

9. *Geschichte* II.106.
1. *Syntax des heutigen Englisch* and *Syntax* respectively.
2. *Syntax* 173.

Ph 1, Soul II 4, Rid 10, Resig 2, ParPs 10, Bo 1, Rune 1, Fasting 1, Beo 2, Jud 1. Apart from these, there are several cases which may be (elliptically) concessive but seem rather adversative, and are therefore discounted.[3] The following examples of concessive *and* are typical:

> Hwilum of heofnum   hate scineð,
> blicð þeos beorhte sunne,   and wit her baru standað,
> unwered wædo.   (Gen 810)
> Sume him þæs hades   hlisan willað
> wegan on wordum   ond þa weorc ne doð.   (Gl 60)

It has been seen in earlier sections that *and* is used frequently to reinforce the more autonomous concessive elements *þeah* and *hwæðere* (II.2, III.1). When *and* is acting as the chief concessive sign it is in turn reinforced several times:

and . . . gyt   ChrSat 405.
and þonne   Ph 552, Rid 28/7.
and(. . .)eft   ParPs 56/8, 105/11.
and(. . .)nu   Dan 757, And 279, 1414, El 663, 664, Chr 185.

A few verbless *and*-members occur, verbless usually by ellipsis:

> Þær wæs eallgylden
> fleohnet fæger . . .
> . . . þæt se bealofulla
> mihte wlitan þurh . . .
> on æghwylcne   þe ðærinne com
> hæleða bearna,   and on hyne nænig
> monna cynnes   (Jud 46)

So also Rid 21/8, Rood 13, Rune 13. But note this example from the prose: 'Gif he moste þa gyt twa gear libban. he hæfde Yrlande mid his werscipe gewunnon. 7 wiðutan ælcon wæpnon' (ASC E 1086). For the most part however *and*-members contain finite verbs, and since these members are notionally apodoses (*and* being a coordinator, not a subordinator like early NE *an(d)*), the mood is unaffected by the concessive relation.

On the whole, there is little that is significant about the word order in concessive *and*-members or that is different from the analysis made by Fourquet.[4] There is considerable variety, but the clear majority have the order *and–subject–object/complement–verb*. About one-third of the examples have the order *subject–verb–etc.*, and there are scattered examples of other variations (*verb–subject–etc.*, for example,

---

3. See the discussion in the section on *ac* above.
4. *L'Ordre des éléments de la phrase* 38ff., 95ff., 182ff.

in ParPs 118/110). There is little evidence in the verse of the tendency noticeable in some prose, to throw a word or phrase essential to the concession into relief by making it follow the *and* immediately, as in: 'Þa ætsæton ða Centiscan þær beæftan ofer his bebod, 7 seofon ærendracan he him hæfde to asend' (ASC A 905).

The strength of *and* as a concessive sign is illustrated by the fact that, whereas we have earlier seen some tendency on the part of OE poets to increase the formal strength of the concessive expression found in their originals, *and* on the other hand often corresponds to a more explicit sign in the original. Thus *ond* in Rid 40/18 corresponds to *rursus*, in 40/44 to *ecce tamen*, in 40/64 to a *cum*-clause; it is worth noting that in the OE version of St. Augustine's *Soliloquies* a concession formed with *and* also translates a *cum*-clause (Burnham, p. 97). But the reverse also occurs; in Bo 20/159 *and þeah* corresponds to *and* in the prose source. Once (Rid 40/31) *ond* translates *nunc* used concessively, twice (ParPs 90/7, 101/23) *and* stands for *autem* in the Latin, and twice also (both in ParPs 93/9) *and*-concessions correspond to concessive-equivalent relative (*qui*) clauses. In Gen 810, *and* corresponds to zero relating element in the OS version:

>   Huilum thanne fan himile   heto skinit,
>   blikit thiu berahto sunna.   Uuit hier thus bara standat,
>   unuuerid mið giuuadi.   (ASPR 1.171)

The only example of concessive *and* in Bo keeps the same construction as in the prose (28/49), and in ParPs five instances of *and* match *et* alone in the Latin (56/8, 61/4, 105/11, 118/110, 134/16), and another concessive *and* owes its existence presumably to a misunderstanding of the nonconcessive Latin context (ParPs 59/3).

The ASC provides particularly interesting material to show the interchangeability of *and* with other concessive elements. In E 755 —'he his feorh generede. 7 he wæs oft gewundod'—7 corresponds to 7 *þeah* in A; in F 887 7 corresponds to *þeah* in A and E. In F 1016 we find 7 for *ac* in D and E; in D 1050 7 for *ac* in C; in C 1065, E 1070 and E 1076 7 for *ac* in D; in D 1050 *ac* is written over 7.

It is important to stress that *and* was apparently felt to be adequate in OE as a means of expressing the concessive relation, since modern editors have not always recognized this. In ChrSat 405, ASPR reads:

>   Let þa up faran   eadige sawle,
>   Adames cyn,   ac ne moste Efe þa gyt
>   wlitan in wuldre

In a footnote we are told that instead of *ac* the manuscript reads *and* "in the usual abbreviated form." In view of the material in this section and especially since *and* is more frequent than *ac* in the concessions of OE poetry, there should be no emendation here, though ASC D 1050 (see above) shows that such an emendation is by no means a modern idea.

In And 629, the manuscript reads:

>   Hwæt frinest ðu me,   frea leofesta,
>   wordum wrætlicum,   ond þe wyrda gehwære
>   þurh snyttra cræft   soð oncnawest?

Bright (MLN ii.163) maintains that we should read *ond þeh*, thus making the concession more explicit: 'Why do you ask me this *and yet* know all along?' Krapp himself so read in his early edition of the poem,[5] but on reflection wisely decided to keep the manuscript reading, saying (ASPR ii.112), "the change is not necessary, since *þe* can be taken as a dative of reference, 'for thyself'."

To sum up the section, *and* is used in OE verse for about 4 per cent of the concessions; it is occasionally reinforced by *gyt, þonne, eft* and *nu*; nondependent members introduced by *and* may sometimes be without finite verbs, but otherwise they have predominantly the word order *subject–object–verb*. The study of other versions of the texts shows the strength of *and* alone as a concessive connective, and throws more light on the range of concessive expressions felt to be of equal effect.

4. *forðon*

The word *forðon* occurs eight times in *The Seafarer*, and in four of these cases the text is difficult to interpret if we give the word its normal causal meaning. For instance:

>   Þæt se beorn ne wat,
>   *esteadig secg,   hwæt þa sume dreogað
>   þe þa wræclastas widost lecgað.
>   Forþon nu min hyge hweorfeþ   ofer hreþerlocan,
>   min modsefa   mid mereflode
>   ofer hwæles eþel hweorfeð wide
>   *MS: eft eadig   (Seaf 55)

The sufferings of the sea traveler seeming a poor reason for putting to sea oneself, scholars have long debated the possibility that *forðon* in such contexts as this may signify *inverted* cause, that is, be a concessive or at least adversative element. This suggestion seems first

---

5. *Andreas and the Fates of the Apostles* (Boston 1906).

to have been made seriously by Rieger,[6] who made it serve his theory that the poem was originally a dialogue, and several other scholars, notably E. A. Kock, M. Daunt, and S. B. Liljegren,[7] have subscribed to the view and advanced evidence in its support. It has been shown that in the Lindisfarne Gospels (*St. John* ix.41), *vero* is glossed by *forþon ł hueþre*, and in other translations from Latin there are scattered examples of *forðon* corresponding to *autem* and *sed* (for example, *Pastoral Care* xxi). Attention has also been drawn to the adversative functions of *for*.

Burnham makes no mention of *forðon* as a concessive element except (p. 31) in so far as it is sometimes correlative to *þeah*, when it has the combined causal and concessive force of 'for all that.' She also notes (p. 115) an occasion in Ælfric where *forðy* has "true concessive meaning."

There is little evidence of a concessive function of *forðon* in OE poetry. There are only three cases outside Seaf where the context allows even the possibility of such an interpretation. Two of them are in Wife:

> Þær ic sittan mot   sumorlangne dæg,
> þær ic wepan mæg   mine wræcsiþas,
> earfoþa fela;   forþon ic æfre ne mæg
> þære modceare   minre gerestan   (Wife 37)

Is the weeping related causally or concessively to the inability to get rid of grief? It is difficult to decide with certainty, but concession is on the whole less likely. Secondly, we have:

> Het mec hlaford min   herheard niman,
> ahte ic leofra lyt   on þissum londstede,
> holdra freonda.   Forþon is min hyge geomor,
> ða ic me ful gemæcne   monnan funde,
> heardsæligne   (Wife 15)

The crux here is *herheard*, MS: *her heard*. Mackie (*Exeter Book* 152) and other editors follow the manuscript division and interpret as 'stern lord,' making the interpretation of the first two lines somewhat difficult. But in 1865, Grein proposed that the manuscript should be read *herheard* (that is, *hearg-eard*), 'grove-dwelling.'[8] This suggestion is accepted in ASPR, and is supported by ll. 27–8:

> Heht mec mon wunian   on wuda bearwe,
> under actreo   in þam eorðscræfe.

6. *Zeit. für deut. Phil.* i.335.
7. *Lunds Univ. Årsskr.* I.xiv(26).75–6, MLR xiii.474–9 and StNeophil xiv.145ff. respectively.
8. 'Zur Textkritik der angelsächsischen Dichter,' *Germania* x.416–29.

This reading would seem to make probable a causal relationship between lines 15 and 16, and *Forþon* is thus possibly concessive: 'My lord bade me take a dwelling in the woods, being so devoid of friends. And yet my heart is sad . . .' But no doubt the sadness may also be reckoned as *deriving from* the lack of friends.

Thirdly, we may consider the following use of *forðon*:

Ic beo fægere beþeaht   fiðerum þinum

. . . . .

me ðin seo swiðre onfencg   symble æt ðearfe.
Forðon hi on idel   ealle syððan
sohton synlice   sawle mine   (ParPs 62/8)

For *Forðon hi* the Latin has *Ipsi vero*, and this may bear an adversative interpretation: 'But in their wickedness they have persisted in vain persecution of my soul.' If however the sentence has *on idel* as its focal point, the *Forðon* is causal: 'In view of thy protection, they have been harrying my soul in vain.'

In the verse outside Seaf we have thus no sure evidence of *forðon* functioning as a concessive element, and since there is still much controversy over the whole interpretation of this poem, it is not easy to be convinced that *forðon* is concessive even in this text. At the beginning of the present century, W. W. Lawrence disposed of the theory that the poem had been composed as a dialogue and convinced many scholars that there was no need to assume that *forðon* has any irregular adversative function in the poem.[9] He is followed by Krapp and Dobbie, who suggest that "it is best to take *Forþon* . . . as a loose connective, without any specific syntactical relationship."[1]

O. S. Anderson, while admitting the plausibility of Kock's comparing (loc.cit.) *forðon* with the ON causal and concessive *fyrir því*, rejects a concessive interpretation chiefly, it seems, on the grounds that in Seaf *forðon* occurs in an unquestionably causal sense (for example, ll. 72, 103, 108), and that it would be odd for the poet to use it also concessively.[2] The apparent truth of this however derives from our thinking (as in translation we must) of *forðon* as usually 'meaning' *therefore*. But translation obscures the fact that to the Anglo-Saxon it meant only *for that*, and *for* certainly had both concessive and causal function just as it has today; 'for all my blessings' is causal or concessive according to whether the context is 'I am thankful' or 'I am not thankful,' and no incongruity would be felt if both senses were used within a single paragraph. Similarly, in Gen 2475f. we find *for* used causally and

---

9. JGPh iv.463ff.
1. ASPR III.296; cf. also Mackie (*Exeter Book*): 'truly.'
2. 'The Seafarer. An Interpretation,' *Kungl. Hum. Vet. i Lund Arsberättelse* 1937–38, p. 8.

concessively in successive lines (see IV.24), and we may also compare Rood, where in the space of the first 70 lines *hwæðere* is used concessively four times and nonconcessively three times.

To S. O. Andrew the *Forþon* of Seaf 58 does not refer back to the previous sentence but forward to the *Forþon* of l. 64 in a causal correlation.[3] He compares the following construction in *Blickling Homilies*: 'Forþon heo fæmne cende forðon heo wæs fæmne geeacnod.' D. Whitelock is inclined to extend this principle to the pair of *forðon*-members in ll. 33ff., 39ff., translating: '(Therefore) my heart's thoughts constrain me to venture on the deep sea . . . because there is no man on earth so high-hearted . . . that he will not always feel anxiety over his voyage.'[4] But even if one were readily convinced that the statements in ll. 33ff. and 58ff. constituted cogent reasons for the statements in ll. 39ff. and 64ff. respectively, it is doubtful whether we should be justified in regarding the rather remotely spaced *forðon* . . . *forðon* in each case as correlative. Correlations in OE are rarely so syntactically involved, a more representative pattern being that in Andrew's quotation from the *Blickling Homilies*.

Since therefore in ll. 33, 39, 58, and 64 *forðon* introduces members the thought content of which is felt naturally to be in considerable concessive contrast to that of the respective preceding members, it would seem reasonable to interpret the *forðon* in these cases as pointing the contrast, especially as there is some evidence—however meager—in translated prose to show that *forðon* could be so used.

5. *mid þy*

Burnham (p. 76) gives a number of quite clear examples of *mid þy* used concessively. The examples are all of *mid þy* as a subordinating conjunction in correlation with *hwæðere* or *swa þeah* in a nondependent member, translating *cum . . . tamen* or *cum . . . vero* in Bede and the *Dialogues* of Gregory. Similarly, Behaghel[5] gives *mit thiu* as a subordinating concessive conjunction in OS.

No such function can be attributed to *mid þy* in the OE poetry, but in one place it seems to be used concessively in a nondependent member. At any rate, *mid þy* here is hardly in its normal temporal function,

---

3. *Syntax and Style* 33.
4. 'The Interpretation of the *The Seafarer*,' *The Early Cultures of North-West Europe* (ed. Sir Cyril Fox and Bruce Dickins, Cambridge 1950) 264. Dr. Whitelock's learned and attractive interpretation does not however depend, as she expressly points out, on this view of the *forðon* problem.
5. *Deutsche Syntax* III.§1424 C.

and Gordon's interpretation of it as causal [6] seems decidedly forced; it could of course be read as purely instrumental, 'thereby,' but a concessive meaning, 'withal,' seems to suit the situation better:

> Lytel þuhte ic leoda bearnum,   læg ic on heardum stane,
> cildgeong on crybbe.   Mid þy ic þe wolde cwealm afyrran,
> hat helle bealu,   þæt þu moste halig scinan
> eadig on þam ecan life   (Chr 1424)

6. *butan*

Although *butan* was to become the most frequent concessive connective in later English, Burnham gives no examples of it in this function in OE prose.[7] Normally the word occupies the same semantic range as *nemne* and its variants, and is concerned with introducing exceptions which bear only that notional closeness to concession that is inherent in the expression of exception. Consider the relationship expressed in Beo 1559 and 1351 where *buton* and *næfne* respectively appear in closely similar contexts. The closeness to concession of some of the exceptions formed with *butan* is shown by the fact that one in ASC A 889 is actually interpreted as a concession by Rübens.[8]

Nevertheless in both poetry and prose we can just see the beginnings of the modern concessive function. OE *butan* was both a subordinating and a coordinating conjunction,[9] and it is in the latter function that it begins to take on its substitutive and concessive meanings. Thus in the prose version of Bo we read, ' Ne gemdon hie nanes fyrenlustes, buton swiðe gemetlice þa gecynd beeodan ' (33/26); in the same text (40/8), *buton* might be again reckoned substitutive were it not for the presence of *þeah*: ' ne ic ealles forswiðe ne girnde þisses eorðlican rices, buton tola ic wilnode þeah . . .'

But it is when *butan* is preceded by a member containing ' know not ' that the exception function seems most overlaid by concession; again in the prose Bo (70/26), there is the example, ' ic nat humeta, buton we witon þ hit unmennisclic dæd wæs '; compare also Oros 17/13. It

---

6. *Anglo-Saxon Poetry* (London 1926) 175.

7. She mentions it however as a concessive and concessive-equivalent preposition (pp. 110, 116); on this function of *butan* in the present material, see below IV.19.

8. *Parataxe und Hypotaxe* 43; the example is, ' næs nan færeld to Rome, buton tuegen hleaperas Ælfred cyning sende.' Since *tuegen hleaperas* constitute a *færeld* of sorts, a concessive relation expressed here even by *and þeah* in place of *buton* could only be due to a logical failure on the writer's part.

9. Cf. Wülfing, *Syntax* II.684–5.

is in such a context that we find the only poetic example of *butan* used as a relating element at all concessively:

>Nat ic hit be wihte,   butan ic wene þus,
>þæt þær screoda wære   gescyred rime
>siex hun(........)a   (Pharaoh 4)

It is clear that *butan* (like the connectives to be discussed in the next few sections) was not autonomously concessive but occasionally *concessive-equivalent*, combining its exception function with a concessive one. On this subject, see IV.10 below, where the main concessive-equivalent constructions are introduced.

7. *gyt(a), gen(a)*

While forms of *yet* appear in some of her examples, Burnham does not draw attention specifically to the concessive function of this word, and it may well be more widespread in OE poetry than in the prose. In the poetry, the concessive function is difficult and often impossible to separate from the temporal one, and even when it is concessive, *gyt* has not usually its modern function as a connective linking nondependent concessive members. Many of the OE concessions with *gyt* are elliptical and many are single-word dependent concessions which are intruders in the present part of the study. It was felt however that it is more useful to group here all concessions formed with *gyt* and *gen* than to obscure the importance of these words by disintegrating their concessive patterns. Moreover, no attempt to separate all the individual types could be satisfactory, as there is much overlapping of form and function, with no clear line of division between those grammatically dependent and those nondependent.

We find *gyt* and *gen* occurring in many forms: *g(i)et(a)*, *git(a)*, *gyt(a)*, *g(i)en(a)*, *gin*, *geno* (Rid 20/29). In giving the distribution of *gyt* and *gen* used with even partial concessive feeling, I add in parentheses the total occurrences of the word, concessive and nonconcessive, in each text:

gyt: Gen 9 (20),[1] Ex 0 (2), ChrSat 2 (5), And 6 (9), Soul 1 1 (1), Rood 1 (1), Chr 1 (2), Gl 1 (1), Resig 1 (1), Hell 0 (1), Ruin 0 (1), ParPs 2 (6), Bo 9 (12), Finn 1 (2), Wald 0 (1), Maldon 2 (2), ASCPoems 3 (3), Sol 1 (2), Menol 1 (1), Exhort 1 (1), Fasting 0 (1), EpMS 41 1 (1), Beo 10 (18), Jud 2 (2).

1. Gen B 1 (2).

gen: Gen 6 (8),² Ex 1 (1), And 4 (4), El 7 (8), Chr 4 (6), Gl 7 (7), Ph 1 (1), Jul 6 (9), Max 1 0 (1), Panther 1 (1), Whale 1 (2), Partridge 0 (1), Rid 3 (5), ParPs 1 (1), Sol 1 (1), Beo 5 (13).

Thus out of a total of 96 occurrences of *gyt*, 55 are used concessively, while for *gen* we have 69 occurrences, 48 of them concessive; although *gen* is used proportionately more than *gyt* for concession, there is no indication that the difference in proportion is significant, and the functions of *gyt* and *gen* within the concessive patterns seem not to differ at all; both enter the same combinations and correlations; they occupy the same semantic range. As with *þeah* and *þeah þe*, we have mainly to do with the preference of individual texts for one or other form: ChrSat, ParPs, and Bo for instance use *gyt* predominantly, while El, Chr, Gl, Jul, and Rid prefer *gen*; and as with *þeah* and *þeah þe*, a few texts—notably Beo—use both about equally. We shall therefore consider them synonymous and refer to them and their by-forms collectively as '*gyt*,' except when special attention needs to be drawn to another form.

As has been indicated, our distinction between the temporal and concessive functions of *gyt* is to a certain extent almost arbitrary. At times the concessive function is quite clear, with little or no temporal significance:

      me wæs a cearu symle
 lufena to leane, swa ic alifde nu.
 Giet biþ þæt *selast, þonne mon him sylf ne mæg
 wyrd onwendan, þæt he þonne wel þolige.
    *MS deest   (Resig 115)

At times the concessive relation is again uppermost, but is intimately woven with a clearly expressed temporal relation as well:

     Ða to þam wage gesag,
 heafelan onhylde, hyrde þa gena
 ellen on innan.   (Gl 1269)

At times the temporal relation is uppermost, but there is just a hint of concession as well; the following example is not from the material reckoned concessive for this study:

     Cyning ure gewat
 þurh þæs temples hrof þær hy to segun,
 þa þe leofes þa gen last *weardedun
 on þam þingstede, þegnas gecorene.
    *MS: wearde dum (Chr 494)

2. Gen B O (1).

Finally we have the purely temporal examples like the following:

> Wit þæt gecwædon   cnihtwesende
> ond gebeotedon   —wæron begen þa git
> on geogoðfeore—   þæt wit on garsecg ut
> aldrum neðdon   (Beo 535)

One of the frequent functions of *gyt* is in 'even' concessions. This function is often helped by grouping *gyt* with *furðor* (see also IV.20) or other comparative forms. Thus:

gyt and *furðor* in the same member:
  ChrSat 224, And 1487, Ph 234, Jul 317, Beo 3006 ('folcred fremede, oððe furður gen eorlscipe efnde').

gyt and *furðor* in different members:
  Gl 1221 ('ic giet ne wat, ær þu me . . . furþor cyðe').

gyt and other comparatives in the same member:
  Chr 190, Gl 517, Panther 25, Whale 49, Rid 40/58, Bo 21/20, 25/64, 28/70, Jud 181 ('monna mæst morðra gefremede . . . and þæt swyðor gyt ycan wolde').

No special form is needed when *gyt* expresses or rather hints at what we may call the 'threatened' concession: 'the brothers were yet at peace,' that is, with the veiled suggestion: 'though later, as we all know, they . . .' For example:

> Ða giet wæs Sethes cynn,
> leofes leodfruman   on lufan swiðe
> drihtne dyre   (Gen 1245)

Compare also Beo 1163. In a passage beginning at Beo 1017, *þenden* is used in a similar context.

In conjunction with specifically concessive elements, *gyt* has already been noticed to some extent in earlier sections.[3] As correlative to subordinating *þeah*, *gyt* occurs in And 474, Gl 515, Jul 191; reinforcing *þeah* in the same member, it occurs in Soul 1 135 (according to the emendation), Bo 23/1, 24/45. Similarly we should note:

gyt and *hwæðere* in the same member:
  Gen 1726, And 51, 1487, Gl 231, 446, Menol 68.

gyt and *hwæðere* in different members:
  Gen 212, 2363, Gl 517.

and and *gyt* in the same member:
  ChrSat 405 (ASPR emends to *ac*).

---

3. See above, II.2, III.2, 3.

Above all, *gyt* is reinforced by various temporal elements, especially *þa* and *nu*; indeed in well over half the total occurrences in the poetry, *gyt* appears in such groups:

þa gyt occurs 43 times
nu gyt occurs 11 times
(n)æfre gyt occurs three times
þonne gena occurs once in ParPs 93/13.

This temporal reinforcement is no guide to the function of the group, which can be just as plainly concessive as unreinforced *gyt*:

     Þær on rime forborn
 þurh þæs fires fnæst fif ond hundseofontig
 hæðnes herges. Ða gen sio halge stod
 ungewemde wlite.   (Jul 587)

These groups are capable also of the 'even' function ('Ða get ic furðor' ChrSat 224), although normally when grouped with comparatives in this function *gyt* is not temporally reinforced. Compare Chr 494, Gl 515.

Concessive *gyt*-phrases without finite verb are not infrequent. For example:

     He hafað oþre gecynd,
 wæterþisa wlonc, wrætlicran gien.   (Whale 49)

Where a finite verb is present, there is no indication that its mood is influenced by the concessive particle or function. In nine-tenths of the examples, the *gyt*-member follows the member with which it is in concessive relation. There are several cases in the poetry however in which it precedes; this is usually when the *gyt* is correlative to *þeah* (for example, Jul 191), or *hwæðere* (for example, Gen 212), in a different member. There are also two examples of the *gyt*-member being placed medially and parenthetically (for example, Rood 28) in the member with which it is in concessive relation.

In two-thirds of the examples, *gyt* and *gyt*-groups like *þa gyt* occupy a medial position in the member; nevertheless there are 34 cases with *gyt* initially. Final position occurs only eight times, though its validity as a stylistic pattern is shown by the following parallel examples:

  . . . he him on heafde helm ær gescer,
 þæt he blode fah bugan sceolde,
 feoll on foldan; næs he fæge þa git (Beo 2973)
      Sloh ða wundenlocc
 þone feondsceaðan . . .

    . . . . .

NONDEPENDENT CONCESSIONS WITHOUT þeah III.8   67

. . . þæt he on swiman læg,
druncen and dolhwund.   Næs ða dead þa gyt
(Jud 103)

In these two cases, of course, *gyt* is predominantly temporal.

There is little to be learnt from the study of originals and parallel versions. In the Latin originals there is either nothing to correspond to *gyt* (Rid 40/58, ParPs 77/23, 93/13), or we find *gyt* straightforwardly rendering *adhuc* (ParPs 77/30).[4] In Bo, *gyt* is used five times (7/1, 13/1,[5] 20/20, 25/64, 28/70) without any corresponding *gyt*-form in the prose. In Bo 17/5 *eac nu get* corresponds to a simple *git* in the prose; in 21/20 only the word order is different: *get swiðor*, which the versifier for metrical reasons changes to *swiðor get*. Where the prose on one occasion has 'we sculon get,' the versifier makes a half-line by using the more explicitly concessive form of expression, 'we sculon ðeah gita' (Bo 23/1); finally, where the prose uses *gyt* in a concessive-equivalent relative clause ('þe ðu nu geot forgiten hafst'), the poet puts it in a dependent *þeah*-member with the subjunctive, 'ðeah ðu hi nu geta forgiten hæbbe' (Bo 24/44).

To sum up, *gyt* (which we cannot distinguish syntactically or semantically from *gen*) occurs in various functions ranging from entirely temporal to entirely concessive, with no clear line of demarcation between these two uses. As well as being the relating element in nondependent concessions, it is frequently used for elliptically dependent concessions, especially of the 'even' kind. It usually takes up medial position in its member which in turn usually follows the member with which it is in concessive relation. It is often associated with more autonomous concessive elements and very frequently it is temporally reinforced, particularly by *þa*.

8. *nu*

We have already seen *nu* assisting concession when grouped with *and* and *gyt* (III.3, 7), and when correlated to *þeah* (II.2); we have now to look at it as the sole concessive sign in nondependent concessions. Burnham (p. 72) indicates its concessive function in relative clauses and (p. 78) in temporal clauses used concessively, and Behaghel[6]

---

4. Cf. *gyt* 'adhuc,' *gyt þeahhwæþere* 'adhuc tamen' in Ælfric's Colloquy ll. 285, 263 respectively (ed. G. N. Garmonsway [London 1938]); in ASC a 449 and 565 simple *gyt* renders Bede's *usque hodie* (Plummer 1.31, 133).

5. In this case, its introduction provides convenient alliteration with *giddum*.

6. *Deutsche Syntax* III.§1424 C.

mentions sporadic dependent member concessions so introduced in OHG also. Neither scholar mentions it in connection with nondependent concessions, but in this function it occurs some 18 times in OE poetry, distributed as follows: Gen 1, Dan 1, ChrSat 2, And 3, Rood 1, El 1, Chr 1, Az 1, RimP 1, Rid 3, ParPs 1, Bo 1, Beo 1. For example:

>   Þæt eower fela geseah,
>   . . . þæt we þry *sendon,
> geboden to bæle   in byrnende
> fyres leoman.   Nu ic þær feower men
> geseo to soðe   *MS: syndon   (Dan 411)

All the examples contain finite verbs the mood of which, since they are in notional apodoses, is not influenced by *nu* or its function. In 13 cases, *nu* takes initial position in its member, in five cases followed by *subject–verb* (ChrSat 151, RimP 38, Rid 71/1, Bo 2/1, Beo 932), but in the remaining examples several patterns are found. In five cases *nu* occupies a medial position, three times preceded only by the verb which thus takes initial place (Rood 80, Chr 820, ParPs 118/69).

There are only two points from Latin originals to consider, but both are of interest. In Rid 40/98, the nondependent concession with *nu* corresponds to a dependent concession with *cum* in Aldhelm's Latin, and in ParPs 118/69 *nu* translates *autem*. In Bo 2/1 *nu* corresponds to *nu* in the prose also, but there the concessive feeling is thrown back on to a preceding relative clause.

9. *þa*

As with *nu*, we have already seen *þa* used to assist in the concessive function of such elements as *gyt*.[7] It is also used alone on a modest scale to introduce nondependent concessive members in OE poetry. There are six examples to be considered, distributed as follows: ChrSat 2, Chr 1, Jul 1, Rid 1, ParPs 1. For example:

> earm ic wæs on eðle þinum   þæt þu *wurde eadig on minum.
> Þa ðu þæs ealles   ænigne þonc
> þinum nergende   nysses on mode.   *MS: worde
>   (Chr 1496)

In each case *þa* introduces its member, the word order of which does not differ from that obtaining when *þa*-members are entirely temporal

---

7. III.7; see also II.2. Again as with *nu*, Burnham (pp. 75, 76) draws attention to the concessive function only of dependent *þa*-members.

in function; there is thus nothing to add to the details given by Fourquet.[8]

In ParPs 77/19, *þa* has its concessive force underlined by *furþur*, and these two elements correspond to the Latin *et . . . adhuc*; compare VespPs 7 . . . *ðaget*. This is the only example in our material for which there is a Latin original, but it is worth mentioning that the manuscripts of ASC provide some interesting points. In E 992 and E 1004 *þa* introducing a nondependent concessive member corresponds to *ac* in F; in F 1051 a concession with *þa* corresponds to one with *þa . . . þeah* in E.

10. *þonne*

Like *þa* and *nu*, *þonne* is used occasionally in conjunction with *þeah* and other concessive elements.[9] Behaghel says that in OHG *thanne* is found occasionally introducing dependent concessions,[1] and Burnham (p. 77) finds *þonne* doing likewise in OE, but neither scholar mentions *þonne* in connection with nondependent concessions. In such concessions it occurs 14 times in the poetic material, distributed as follows: Gen (B) 1, Wand 1, Deor 1, ParPs 9, Bo 1, Sol 1. For example:

> Næs him on hreðre   heorte clæne,
> ne hi on gewitnesse   wisne hæfdon,
> on hiora fyrhþe   fæstne geleafan.
> He þonne is mildheort   and manðwære
> hiora fyrendædum   (ParPs 77/36)

There is one member without finite verb:

> Lytle hwile   sceolde he his lifes niotan,
> secan þonne landa   sweartost on fyre.   (Gen 486)

The word order within the *þonne*-member is interesting enough to warrant being described in detail. Only three times does *þonne* take initial position, once followed by *verb–subject* (Wand 41), once by *subject–verb* (Sol 314), and once by *subject–object* with the verb at the end (ParPs 70/19). In Bo 25/22 *þonne* is the third word in its member and comes between subject and verb. In the remaining 10 examples *þonne* is the second word in its member; three times it is preceded by the verb and followed immediately by the object (Gen 486,

---

8. *L'Ordre des éléments* 102ff., 176ff.
9. See II.2, III.3, 7.
1. *Deutsche Syntax* III.§1424 C.

Deor 28, ParPs 125/5); seven times it is preceded by the subject alone: ParPs 77/36, 81/6, 88/33, 101/23, 51/6, 58/15, 68/12; in the first four of these the verb immediately follows, while in the last three it is placed at the end. Thus out of nine occurrences in ParPs, *þonne* once stands at the head of its member and eight times takes second position; it can hardly be a coincidence that in the one case *þonne* corresponds to *et conversus*, while in the other eight it translates *autem* or *vero*, which each time occurs in the Latin in second position. The Latin seems to have had a distinct influence on the word order of the OE version in this respect.

The details of the Latin correspondences are as follows: *þonne* renders *autem* in ParPs 51/6, 58/15, 77/36, 81/6, 101/23, and 125/5; it renders *vero* in ParPs 68/12, 88/33, and corresponds to *et conversus* in ParPs 70/19. The OE prose source of Bo 25/22 has *ac . . . þonne* where the poet uses simply *þonne*.

II. MINOR RELATING ELEMENTS

There are several nondependent concessions in which the relation is not pointed by any of the elements so far presented. At the same time it is impossible in some cases and it would be unwise in the others to say that there was no relating element or that certain elements present in the concessions do not assist the relation.

Burnham (p. 30) finds that *huru* " is not infrequently correlative " to *þeah*, and we have seen it in that function in the poetic material (II.2). It is therefore right to draw attention to it when it is the only possible relating element in three concessions: Chr 785, Hell 11, Beo 857. For example:

>   Sohton sarigu tu   sigebearn godes
>   ænne in þæt eorðærn   þær hi ær wiston
>   þæt hine gehyddan   hæleð Iudea;
>   wendan þæt he on þam beorge   bidan sceolde,
>   ana in þære easterniht.   Huru þæs oþer þing
>   wiston þa wifmenn,   þa hy on weg cyrdon!   (Hell 11)

Similarly, the interjection *hwæt* seems to be the concessive pointer in two instances: Chr 1421, Beo 1769. Thus:

>   Mec mon folmum biwond,
>   biþeahte mid þearfan wædum,   ond mec þa on þeostre alegde
>   biwundenne mid wonnum claþum.   Hwæt, ic þæt for
>   worulde geþolade!   (Chr 1421)

NONDEPENDENT CONCESSIONS WITHOUT þeah III.11   71

There are three concessions occurring close to each other in the *Exeter Book* in which the connecting and relating element is clearly *swylce*: Rid 40/58, 92, Wife 42.

>   Ic eom on goman   gena swetra
>   þonne þu beobread   blende mid hunige;
>   swylce ic eom wraþre   þonne wermod sy   (Rid 40/58)

In this case, Aldhelm connects with *et rursus*, but in the original of the other example (Rid 40/92) we find simply *et*.

There seems to be a single instance of *þær* used as a concessive connective (compare Burnham, p. 78f.) :

>   Þa com ærest Cam   in siðian,
>   eafora Noes,   þær his aldor læg,
>   ferhðe forstolen.   Þær he freondlice
>   on his agenum fæder   are ne wolde
>   gesceawian   (Gen 1577)

In Gl 142, the bold attitude of the devils to Guðlac before his conversion and their retreat afterward are concessively related, the only possible relating element being *þonan*. In the same poem (Gl 907), the contrast between the evil plots of the devils and the unshakable endurance of the saint is concessively pointed by *symle*. In the following example *eft* seems to act as the relating element, though the member so introduced corresponds closely to some with zero relating element (see below, III.12) :

>   Noe tealde   þæt he on neod hine,
>   gif he on þære lade   lande ne funde,
>   ofer sid wæter   secan wolde
>   on wægþele.   Eft him seo wen geleah   (Gen 1443)

All the previous elements in this section have appeared in the second member of a concession. We conclude now with the single instance of *efne* in the first member, pointing to a concessive relation with the following member:

>   Efne hi habbað on muðe   milde spræce,
>   is him on welerum   wrað sweord and scearp.
>   (ParPs 58/7)

The Latin has *ecce*.

To sum up, the minor relating elements which we have seen associated with nondependent concessions are *huru* (3x), *swylce* (3x), *hwæt* (2x), *þær* (1x), *eft* (1x), *þonan* (1x), *symle* (1x), and *efne* (1x).

12. ZERO RELATING ELEMENT

It is clear from the previous section that the line may be hard to draw between minor relating elements and no relating element at all. Nor, except for the bureaucratic matter of classification, may it be of any moment that a member introduced by *þonan* was put into the last section, and several introduced by *þæs, no þy ær* are put into this.[2] But indeed the question may be asked whether true parataxis—that is, the conscious association of two members without a specific relating element—really exists. There is no formal boundary, says Schubiger,[3] between coordination and subordination, and no fundamental difference between them either; what boundary there is, is psychological and conveyed by intonation. Even if we leave out of account what Bloomfield[4] calls 'secondary phonemes' (which are in fact probably never absent from speech, however impossible it may be to recapture them in written forms of a language), we are left with recurrent patterns which themselves may as a whole constitute the relating element. We shall be examining in this section a few such patterns, which appear to have become regularized as the vehicles of concession. Perhaps, one feels, it might be safer not to press our classification beyond Sandmann's basic distinction between 'broken' and 'fluent' forms.[5]

Certainly, it appears that grammarians have differed widely in their attitude to the conventional distinction between parataxis and hypotaxis. Many, like Behaghel, Lerch, Williams, and Wilde, are not concerned with analyzing grammatically, but are content, upon varying amounts and kinds of evidence, to express a genetic relationship between them; to speak, that is, of the 'progress' from parataxis to hypotaxis. "... Prinzipiell aber gilt, dass alle Hypotaxe immer erst aus der Parataxe entstanden ist."[6] Others differ widely in their use of the terms. To Curme (*Syntax* 170) we have parataxis when there is relationship between members but no formal link. Wendt, Jespersen, and Glunz take the same view. On the other hand, Poutsma expressly equates parataxis with coordination, using the term to cover members linked by *and, but, therefore*;[7] similarly, Rübens has members in parataxis

---

2. In point of fact, the distinction drawn here is between a word *only* referring back to a previous member and one which *also* looks forward into the content of its own.
3. 'English Intonation and Syntax' 91f.
4. *Language* (London 1935) 90–2.
5. See ArchLing ii.24–28.
6. Lerch, *Hist.franz.Synt.* I.45. Cf. however Hirt, *Handbuch des Urgermanischen* III.187, and Sandmann, loc.cit.
7. *Grammar* I.II.544.

connected by 'conjunctions of logical relation,' thus making it necessary for him to distinguish between conjunctive and asyndetic parataxis.[8]

"It is to be observed," says Onions, "that, when two sentences are placed side by side in parataxis, one of them must necessarily be subordinated in thought to the other. Therefore, in every instance of parataxis there is virtual, though not formal, hypotaxis."[9] Nils Bøgholm, on the other hand, denies that we have parataxis at all "in cases where one of the two sentences is subordinated in meaning, although there may be no linguistic echo of the relationship."[1] The classical scholar, E. P. Morris, however, has clearly shown that parataxis cannot be argued out of existence in this way. To put entirely independent sentences together like 'The sun is shining,' 'Homer wrote the *Iliad*,' shows, he says, mental disorder. In fact, when such a sequence is uttered, "the normal mind . . . instinctively gropes" for some situation which will give a rational connection, "so strong is the habit of associating mere succession with relation." So far then from beginning with complete notional independence, parataxis to Morris "covers all that lies between coördination and the suggestion of relation by musical means, as the upper limit, and the expression of relation by subordinating words as the lower limit."[2]

In this study, 'parataxis' is nearer to Curme's concept than to Morris' and Poutsma's; hence, for the sake of clarity the alternative term, 'zero relating element.'

Paratactic expression of the concessive relationship is moderately widespread. Lerch gives examples from Latin and French:

Ne sit summum malum dolor, certe est malum.
Je vivrai dix mille ans, je n'oublierai pas un seul détail de cette scène.[3]

We shall see further Latin examples in the source study below. In NE, while parataxis is frequent in the conditional relation ('do it; you'll never regret it') and the causal ('hurry up; it's getting late.' 'It's raining; I'll get my umbrella'), it seems to be less frequent in concession: 'laugh as much as you like; I'm going.' 'I told him he was wrong; he wouldn't believe me.'

It has been noted by Rübens and Glunz that parataxis is much rarer in OE prose than in the verse;[4] Burnham has no section devoted to paratactic concession, making only a passing reference (p. 108) to

---

8. *Parataxe und Hypotaxe* 8, 31.
9. *Advanced English Syntax* §294. Cf. also Kellner, *Historical Outlines* §98f.
1. *The Layamon Texts* 85.
2. *On Principles and Methods* 117, 147.
3. *Hist.franz.Synt* 1.45–6. For MHG examples, see Mensing, *Untersuchungen* 5, 10ff.
4. *Parataxe und Hypotaxe* 8; *Verwendung des Konjunktivs* 58.

an " example of the baldest juxtaposition " in ASC. In OE poetry, on the other hand, there are considerably more concessions formed without relating element than with subordinating *þeah* (*þe*) and not many less than the total concessions, dependent and nondependent, formed with *þeah*. There are 234 cases in which the concessive relation seems quite certain, and they are distributed as follows: Gen 13 (none in Gen B), Ex 2, Dan 5, ChrSat 5, And 16, Fates 1, HomFrag I 3, Rood 1, El 8, Chr 5, Gl 22, Ph 1, Jul 8, Wand 2, Prec 1, Vain 2, Max I 2, RimP 1, Soul II 1, Deor 7, Wulf 1, Rid 31, Wife 1, Jud I 3, Resig 2, Hell 2, Pharaoh 1, HomFrag II 1, Ruin 1, ParPs 40, Bo 3, Maldon 4, ASC Poems 1, Sol 3, Jud II 1, FragPs 1, Prayer 1, Fasting 1, EpPastoral 1, Charm 1, Beo 25, Jud 3. For example:

      Ðu eart seolfa geong,
wigendra hleo, nalas wintrum frod,
hafast þe on fyrhðe, faroðlacende,
eorles ondsware.   (And 505)
He fela findeð, fea beoð gecorene. (Gl 59)
he sunu wyrceð, bið him sylfa fæder. (Rid 37/8)
oft me fuhtan to fynd on geoguþe,
ne mihton hi awiht æt me æfre gewyrcean.
            (ParPs 128/1)
     Heorot eardode,
sincfage sel sweartum nihtum;—
no he þone gifstol gretan moste,
maþðum for Metode, ne his myne wisse. (Beo 166)[5]

The interpretation of the concessive relation, often fraught with the danger of too subjective a judgment, presents particularly great dangers and difficulties in the examples without relating element. " The language has never depended upon the semantic content of its connective words to direct the attention from one clause to another," [6] and whatever difficulties this may give the descriptivist studying current speech, they are nothing compared with those encountered by students of written language. We must have enough of the context to grasp not only the whole situation, but often the writer's attitude to it as well, for the relation as Horn tells us " steckt nicht in den Worten, sondern in der Sache." [7] Even with these precautions one is sometimes

---

5. Although the difficulties of ll. 168-9 have never been entirely solved, it seems clear that those scholars are right who take *he* as Grendel and consider that the poet is contrasting Grendel's unwelcome activities in the hall with a retainer's privileges. See E. A. Kock's lively notes in Anglia xxvii.225-6 and *Lunds Univ. Arsskr.* I.xiv (26).7-8, as well as Wyatt and Chambers, ed., 11f., Klaeber, ed., 134f., 453.

6. Small, JEGPh xxxvii.292.

7. 'Untersuchungen' 217.

unable to decide, and one frequently finds the interpretations of others quite different from one's own. Among others, Glunz several times mistakes other relationships for paratactic concession, for example, 'þær git . . . glidon ofer garsecg; geofon yðum weol' (Beo 515)[8] which seems quite plainly a relation of attendant circumstances. The greatest difficulty is in distinguishing concession from the purely adversative;[9] some adversative relations are easily distinguished, as for example, 'Well is it for him who does good; woe to him who does evil' (cf. Seaf 106, Vain 72), but there are no fewer than 52 examples where it is impossible to say decisively whether the relation is concessive, adversative, or even causal. These dubious cases are not of course counted in the present survey, but their existence is important to note in considering the widespread use of parataxis in the poetry.

As with other forms of concession, elliptical concessions are not infrequent where there is no relating element. For example:

>   Hie wæron reowe,   ræsdon on sona
>   gifrum grapum.   Hine god forstod,
>   staðulfæst steorend, þurh his strangan miht.
>   (And 1334)

The actual concession here, 'Although they tried to destroy him, they could not because God protected him,' is not given expression.

'Even' concession is also conveyed without specific relating element. For example, Beo 2122, El 640; in the latter case, the whole of Elene's speech makes it seem almost certain that in OE the function was assisted in expression by intonation.

There are numerous nondependent members in this section without finite verb. The closeness of the two members to each other and the frequent parallelism of syntactical pattern make ellipsis of the second verb (and other parts of the sentence) very easy:

>   Þær folcstede   fægre wæron,
>   men arlease,   metode laðe.   (Gen 1933)
>   Đa wæs Guðlace, on þa geocran tid
>   mægen gemeðgad, mod swiþe heard,
>   elnes anhydig.   (Gl 976)

So too, HomFrag 1 18, El 386, Prec 5, Deor 32, Wulf 3, Rid 30/1, 33/5, 66/1, 85/3.

There is nothing uncommon in any period of the language about concessions being made to interlock with each other, so that, for example, the protasis of one concession may become the apodosis of a

---

8. *Verwendung des Konjunktivs* 58.
9. See the discussion above in the section on *ac*, III.2.

following one: 'She gave him the book although she grudged him it even though she liked him.' Consider the cultivated nature of the following example: "'Liberty' is not a name for anything nor a descriptive phrase for anything, though it is used as if it were, but sentences in which it occurs can be translated into sentences using only genuine proper names and descriptive phrases."[1] Here, the dependent *though*-member is the protasis and the 'Liberty' member the apodosis in one concessive relationship, and at the same time the 'Liberty' member is notionally the protasis of the main concession in which 'but sentences . . .' is the apodosis.

Mixed, double, or 'chain' concessions occur a good deal in OE with all types of construction:

```
       Hu mæg ænig man    andsware findan
       ðinga æniges,      þegen mid gesceade,
       þeah hine rinca hwile   rihtwislice
       æfter frigne    gif he awuht nafað
       on his modsefan    mycles ne lytles
       *rihtwisnesse    ne geradscipes?
       Nis þeah ænig man    þætte ealles swa
       þæs geradscipes    swa bereafod sie
       þæt he andsware    ænige ne cunne
       findan on ferhðe,    gif he frugnen bið.
           *MS: rihtwisnesses                    (Bo 22/43)
       Bold wæs betlic,    bregorof cyning,
                . . . Hygd swiðe geong,
       wis welþungen,    þeah ðe wintra lyt
       under burhlocan    gebiden hæbbe,
       Hæreþes dohtor;    næs hio hnah swa þeah,
       ne to gneað gifa                          (Beo 1925)
```

But it seems to be particularly frequent with paratactic concessions, a typical pattern being to have the second member of a paratactic concession act as the first member of a formally expressed concession. For example:

```
                    Fell hongedon
       sweotol ond gesyne    on seles wæge
       anra gehwylces.    Ne wæs hyra ængum þy wyrs,
       ne *siðe þy **sarre,    þeah hy swa sceoldon
       reafe birofene
            *MS: side  **MS: sarra               (Rid 13/3)
```

Again, the type of concession which has a verb expressing some

---

1. C. K. Ogden, *Bentham's Theory of Fictions* (London 1932) li (note).

kind of volition in the first member, followed by a renunciation of its action in the second, is widespread in all constructions, but seems especially common where there is no relating element. Thus:

> Heton lædan ut
> þrohtheardne þegn þriddan siðe,
> woldon aninga ellenrofes
> mod gemyltan. Hit ne mihte swa! (And 1390)
> Woldun hy geteon mid torncwidum
> earme aglæcan in orwennysse,
> meotudes cempan. Hit ne meahte swa! (Gl 574)[2]

Musical factors may well have contributed to the expression of the short second member of these concessions.

In this category too we must reckon the disjunctive pattern, 'Him seo wen geleah,' which we shall be examining below in the discussion of word order. But the short, pithy second member is of still wider currency in paratactic concessions; in Chr 1379 we have: 'Hwæt, ic þec ... ærest geworhte, ond þe ondgiet sealde ... þu þæs þonc ne wisses.' Compare also RimP 75 and many others.

Another recurring form particularly marked in concession without relating element is the positive nondependent member opposed to a following negative one (cf. above, II.8). Frequently, the effect is emphasized by placing the negative particle—which often has the strong form—at the head of the second member; we shall see more of this type too in the discussion of word order below. The significance of negative members has been noted by Andrew: "Normally ... a *ne*-clause after an affirmative sentence has a particular shade of meaning which may be rendered by an adverbial phrase introduced by 'without' e. g., Ic þa hine lange beseah ne ic hine oncnawan mihte 'I then looked at him for a long time without being able to recognize him.'" Thus, he renders Ælfric's sentence (*Lives of Saints* 1.16.112) 'Seo sawul bið betere ne heo ne undergæð lichamlice mycelnis' as 'The soul is better, though without bodily increase,' and interprets in the same way the similar constructions in *Beowulf*.[3] Andrew seems to be generalizing on too little evidence, however, when he goes on from this to suggest[4] that on the odd occasions in Beo when these members are introduced by *na* and *no* it is due to scribal error. We shall see presently that, quite apart from introductory phrases like *no þy ær*, *no þy sel*, there are plenty of instances of *no* introducing the second member of concessions.

---

2. Cf. 'hyt ne mihte swa' in this function again in Beo 2091.
3. *Syntax and Style* 66f.
4 Op.cit.67; cf. *Postscript* 46.

The word order of the first member of paratactic concessions does not differ from the word order of other nondependent members, and is therefore not significant. There is considerable interest on the other hand in the word order of the second member. There are four main types. With a verb standing at the head of the member, there are 10 examples; with disjunctive order, there are 43 examples; with a negative particle standing at the head, there are 75 examples; the rest of the material (over 100 cases) observes the normal order for nondependent members: *subject–object–verb* or *subject–verb–object*.

1. *Verb initially.* For example: 'wæs him seo gelyfed' Gl 209; 'is þæs gen fela to secgenne' Gl 536; 'Biþ þæs oþer swice' Vain 28. So too, Soul II 97, Rid 25/5, 34/5, 65/5, Resig 52, ParPs 55/3, Bo 20/238.

2. *Disjunctive.* The effect of this type is to throw into relief by placing in initial position a word which is particularly important for the concessive relation. This may be a *proper name* as genitive complement (for example, 'Caines ne wolde tiber sceawian' Gen 978), a *noun* as object (as in 'welan ne benohton beornas' And 1159), an *adjective* (as in 'hnescre ic eom' Rid 40/80), an *adverb* (as in 'Earge ge þæt læstun' Chr 1502), an *infinitive* (as in 'findan ic ne mihte' ParPs 68/20). Other examples are: And 708, 1259, Gl 505, Wife 21, Dan 230, Rid 40/74, ParPs 74/9, 100/5, Maldon 162, DeathAlfred 11, Sol 243, Charm 2/9, Beo 2596. Almost worth putting into a separate class is the disjunctive type which places a *pronoun* initially. The verb may then follow immediately, as in 'Him fylston wel gystas sine' Gen 2486, 'me is snægl swiftra' Rid 40/70; so too, Gen 2630, Ex 452, ParPs 72/1, Jul 227. Or the verb may come at the end, as in 'Him seo wen geleah' Gen 49, a half-line which occurs in the same function also in And 1074 and Beo 2323,[5] ' Eow þær wyrs gelomp' Gl 665 and (with only the pronoun different) ChrSat 24, 'him wiht ne speow' Jud 274 and Beo 2854, 'Hine god forstod' And 1143, 1335 and (only slightly different) 1540, Vain 65, 'Hine se cwealm ne þeah' Jul 605 and (only slightly different) ChrSat 575. Other examples are: Dan 523, ChrSat 370, And 1322, El 365, Jul 203, Beo 2333. The parallelism in word as well as in pattern is important; the distribution is also to be noted; it is especially popular in the 'religious epic.'[5a]

---

5. Cf. also Gen 1446 (see above, III.11).

5a. On the whole question of word patterning in OE verse, see Francis P. Magoun, Jr., 'Oral-Formulaic Character of Anglo-Saxon Narrative Poetry,' *Speculum* xxviii. 446–67.

3. *Negative particle initially.* The material here is best considered in three groups: first, the member introduced by the particle *ne* or *n-* in agglutination with verbal parts; secondly, by *no, na, nawiht, nalles*; and thirdly, by the *no þy sel* type of group.

Initial *ne* is usually followed immediately by the verb and is sometimes agglutinized with it, as in ' Ne wolde him beorht fæder bearn ætniman' Ex 415, ' Nyle he . . . ealle gesyllan' Chr 683, and similarly Dan 143, And 230, 1125, Fates 98, Rood 46, El 491, Gl 325, 353, 465, Jul 506, RimP 75, Rid 13/3, 39/5, 65/1, Jud 1 7, Hell 62, ParPs 58/10, 68/20, 73/20, 80/11, 113/13, 14, 15, 118/61, 83, 128/1, 134/16, 18, 138/9, Maldon 62, 68, 169, Sol 330, 391, FragPs 19, Fasting 160, EpPastoral 18, Beo 2275, ?2296, 2625, 2973, Jud 57, 103. The exceptions, in which *ne* is followed by the subject or other nominal form, are few: ' Ne he sorge wæg' Gl 1137, and similarly Rid 31/12, ParPs 58/3, 77/64, 105/19, 134/17.

Initial *no* on the other hand is always followed by nominal elements, with the verb coming at the end of the member. In connection with Andrew's suggestion noted above that initial *no* in Beo is an error for *ne*, it may be pointed out that we have several examples of this outside Beo. For instance, Gl 266, 406, 412, 547 ('No hy . . . deman moston,' compare Beo 166 'no he . . . gretan moste'), Ph 257, Rid 93/17, ParPs 118/85. Compare also Gl 505, where the *no* is displaced by disjunction: ' soþfæstra no mod ond monþeaw mæran willað.'

An example of the second member introduced by *nawiht* is ' nose habbað, nawiht gestincað' ParPs 134/17; *nalles* is used only once: ' nalles for torne tearas feollon ' El 1133.

With initial *no þy sel* and similar groups, we may compare the way in which *þy* and a comparative are sometimes correlated with *þeah*, as we have seen above (II.2; for example, ' Þeah . . . , hwæt . . . þy bet . . . ?' Bo 10/63), and also such groups as *na þy læs* which occurs as an autonomous concessive element in OE prose.[6] Twice in Beo (2160, 2466) *no þy ær* is itself correlated to a dependent *þeah*-member. The examples of this type of word group introducing the second member of a paratactic concession (if indeed we are justified in denying that the groups are specific relating elements [7]) are as follows: ' no þy sel ' Dan 488, ' no þy forhtra ' Gl 201, ' no þy heanre ' Rid 39/9, ' no þy ær '

---

6. To be compared also are the 'correlated comparison concessions,' IV.17.

7. Paratactic interpretation is supported, for one thing, by the fact that *þy* and a comparative occur in zero relating element concessions, apart from the *no þy sel* type; cf. ' Ne . . . þy wyrs ' Rid 13/5 and note also Beo 2277.

Beo 754, 1502, 2081 (where it is reinforced by *þa gen*), 2160, 2373. Andrew suggests that we add Beo 2124 to this list on the ground that *noðer* is probably a scribal error for *no ðy ær*.⁸ On the *no þy* . . . pattern, see further Burnham, pp. 31 f.

4. *Normal word order.* Despite the importance of the foregoing patterns, it must be stressed that for more than two-fifths of the concessions formed with no relating element the word order of both members is the ordinary one for nondependent members. For example:

Ic eorþan eom	æghwær brædre,	
ond widgielra	þonne þes wong grena;	
folm mec mæg bifon	ond fingras þry	
utan eaþe	ealle ymbclyppan.	(Rid 40/50)
He mec þær on innan	unsynnigne,	
dior dædfruma	gedon wolde	
manigra sumne;	hyt ne mihte swa	(Beo 2089)

By very definition as it were, members with no relating element do not use the subjunctive to express the relationship. Where inversion of subjunctive verb and subject appears in a concessive member with no other relating factor, this is properly to be called 'asyndetic hypotaxis' rather than 'parataxis,' and the single example in my material is therefore reserved for later discussion (IV.3). Occasionally in the present material we have the concession expressed with the imperative⁹ out of which in the opinion of some scholars the 'challenge' (*Herausforderung*) function of the subjunctive originally developed in concessions.¹ Compare NE 'Let him go—I don't care,' and the frequent use in sub-standard speech of the type, 'To hell with him—I'm taking it.' In OE we have:

Hafa arna þanc,	þara þe þu unc bude!	
Wit be þisse stræte	stille þencað	
sæles bidan		(Gen 2437)

---

8. *Syntax and Style* 71; cf. his similar suggestion concerning Beo 972, 1907, *Postscript* 84. While his grammatical arguments in favor of emendation are attractive enough, one can hardly agree that such an error would arise through the rarity of *no þy ær*. Even if the phrase is unknown outside Beo, its recurrence half a dozen times in this poem, not to speak of similar constructions like *no þy leng* 974, makes it unlikely that *both* of the scribes would be led astray by unfamiliarity with it.

9. On the similar use of the imperative in MHG, see Mensing, *Untersuchungen* 11.

1. Cf. Glunz, *Verwendung* 53f., Wilmanns, *Deutsche Grammatik* III.I.261. Also see below, IV.5, 7f., and note the use of *lochu* in indefinite concessions of place, for example ASC E 1009.

NONDEPENDENT CONCESSIONS WITHOUT þeah III.12

>   Hafa þe wunden gold
> þæt ær agen wæs   ussum folce,
> feoh and frætwa!   Læt me freo lædan
> eft on eðel   æðelinga bearn,
> on weste wic   wif and cnihtas,
> earme wydewan!   (Gen 2128)

There are several similar cases.

In considering the original versions behind OE texts we have seen in a previous section that a nondependent concession using *swa þeah hwæðere* (ParPs 118/157) translates a concession expressed without relating element in the Latin, as also does a dependent member introduced by *þeah þe* in ParPs 113/16. In the present material we find some OE paratactic concessions corresponding to similar constructions in the Latin; thus Rid 40/46, ParPs 118/83, 95, 155. Sometimes, too, the OE second member with initial *ne* translates a member similarly introduced in the Latin; thus ParPs 58/3 (*neque*), 58/10 (*ne*). But more frequently, where the OE member begins with the negative particle, the Latin links with *et*; thus ParPs 118/61, 134/16, 17 (twice), 18. Twice the Latin introduces the second member with *etenim*: ParPs 57/1, 128/1; once with a *quia*-clause: ParPs 138/9; once *sic* is a relating element in the Latin where the OE (Rid 40/74) has none. Occasionally too the concessive feeling seems to have been introduced into the OE where there is none in the original; thus ParPs 73/20, 91/4, 100/5, 101/6. There are several cases where the OE paratactic construction renders a more formally expressed concession:

ParPs	54/12	þu eart	Latin:	tu vero
"	54/23	ic me . . .	"	ego vero
"	55/3	wene ic	"	" "
"	118/70	ic . . .	"	" "
"	118/87	ic . . .	"	" "
"	72/1	me . . . syndon	"	mei autem
"	102/16	þin mildheortnes	"	misericordia autem
"	103/27	gif . . . ansyne	"	avertente autem . . . faciem
"	105/32	hi hine	"	ipsi autem
"	118/51	ic þinre æ	"	a lege autem
"	140/7	ele synfulra	"	oleum autem
Rid	40/80	hnescre ic eom	Aldhelm: sed	
"	65/6	sindan . . . monige	Symphosius 44: sed sunt . . . multi	
ParPs	118/85	na ic . . .	Latin: sed non	

Rid	40/52	folm mec	Aldhelm:	et tamen
"	40/70	me is snægl	"	" "
"	40/56	*ic *eom Ulcanus	"	cum (clause)
		**MS desunt		

Finally, the three paratactic concessions in Bo correspond as follows to the prose original. Corresponding to Bo 1/39, the prose has an *ac* construction; corresponding to 4/29, the prose has a concession without relating element; there is no concession in the prose corresponding to 20/241.

To sum up, concessions formed without relating element are frequent in OE poetry. Notionally, the concessive types do not differ from those formed with other constructions; elliptical concession occurs and so too the 'even' type. Commonly, a verb implying volition in the first member is met with a renunciation of its action in the second member, which is often brief and pithy, while its syntactical closeness to the previous member often makes ellipsis of the verb natural. The second member of a paratactic construction is sometimes made the first member of a more formally expressed concession. Certain patterns of word order in the second member of paratactic concessions stand out; an initial negative particle seems especially significant and so does disjunctive word order where a word important to the concession is disjoined from the normal syntactic sequence and made prominent in initial position. As regards mood, the vast majority of these concessions are expressed with the indicative, but occasionally the imperative is found. The study of sources has much interest, particularly when it shows OE translators replacing formally expressed concessions by paratactic ones.

IV

Dependent Concessions Without *þeah*

1. GENERAL

HERE again the danger of blurring our study of the constructions can best be avoided by classifying the concessions by the *form* they take. Some attempt will also be made to group the material, where structurally convenient, according to the notional basis of the concessions. Thus we begin by gathering together the alternative concessions, the inversion construction, the 'whoso' type and others—those called by Kruisinga 'open' concessions. But though other constructions might be considered to belong here (the 'even' concessions formed by single words and phrases, for example), their type of structure makes it more appropriate to group them with formally similar types later. It will be noticed that the concessions here are for the most part classified in a different way from those of the previous chapter; while those were dealt with by individual connectives, these are classified rather by whole syntactical patterns.

2. ALTERNATIVE CONCESSIONS

By an 'alternative concession' we understand one that makes a specific attempt to remove in advance all possible threats to the validity of the utterance to which it is related; it 'excludes all exceptions,' as Glunz puts it.[1] 'Please come, wet or dry.' It is a frequent concessive type, and in NE as in OE there may or may not be a verb in the concessive member which is nonetheless invariably dependent grammatically: 'Sooner or later, fogs always lift' (Harold Brighouse, *Alison's Island*), 'and later on you won't even care whether he comes or not' (Jenny). The word 'alternative' must not be too strictly interpreted; the effort to cover all eventualities may bring in more than the two opposites normally cited:

---

[1]. *Verwendung des Konjunktivs* 56.

> ' Is the foreman in? '
> ' Do you mean the manager? '
> ' Foreman, overseer, manager, director, boss—is he in? '

The construction is classified and characterized in widely different ways by modern grammarians. Kruisinga aptly calls it one of the ' open ' types of concession,[2] while Onions [3] classes it among his ' equivalents ' of the concessive clause; its nearness to the conditional relation is reflected in Poutsma's term ' alternative hypothesis ' (also called ' disjunctive concession ').[4] Indeed, Jespersen [5] goes so far as to classify what he pertinently calls ' clauses of indifference ' not with concession at all but with condition.

The alternative concession in the older forms of the Germanic languages has been discussed by several scholars. Behaghel gives the following example of it from the medieval German *Kutrun*: ' ez regente oder ez snite, wê was ie den vil edelen kinden.' [6] In Burnham's study this type of concession is the main subject of two excellent chapters on ' disjunctive concessive clauses ' and ' inverted concessive clauses.' The OE construction has also been examined by Glunz (op.cit.56f.), but Burnham's remains the only serious and extensive treatment. She finds that ' shortness ' is a characteristic of the idiom (p. 37), draws attention to the ' regular parallelism ' in the construction (p. 47) and to its connection with indefinite concessions of the type ' no matter what . . .' The forms of the construction that she has found in the prose are *sam . . . sam* (p. 35f.), *swa . . . swa . . . swæðer* (p. 38f.), *beo he . . . beo he* (p. 44f.), *wille we nelle we* (p. 48), *oððe, ne* and *ge . . . ge* (p. 117f.). We shall find some interesting differences between this prose usage and that of the poetry.

Alternative concessions are distributed as follows in OE poetry, where they occur 57 times: Gen 5 (none in Gen B), Ex 2, And 1, Soul I 3, El 7, Chr 13, Gl 4, Jul 3, Wand 1, Wid 1, Soul II 1, Jud I 2, Rid 1, ParPs 1, Bo 3, Sol 1, Menol 1, Exhort 1, Prayer 1, PrefDialogues 1, Beo 3, Jud 1. For example:

> Ne mæg ænig þam
> flæsce bifongen   feore wiðstondan,
> ricra ne heanra   (Gl 993)
> Wyrc þæt þu wyrce,   word oððe dæda,
> hafa metodes ege   on gemang symle   (Exhort 16)

Besides the unquestionably concessive examples, we find the frequent

---

2. *Handbook* Part II.§1950.
3. *Advanced English Syntax* §58b.
4. *Grammar* I.II.716.
5. *Mod.Engl.Gr.* v.21.77; ' System of Clauses ' 167.
6. *Deutsche Syntax* III.§1423 B. Cf. also Mensing, *Untersuchungen* 16ff.

occurrence of a grouping of opposites in a similar way but probably without concessive relation. For example:

> Ge neh ge feor   is þin nama halig   (And 542)
> Hwæt! We feor and neah   gefrigen habað
> ofer middangeard   Moyses domas   (Ex 1)

There is clearly an essential difference between the all-embracing inclusiveness of the general statement in these examples (which seem to be a rhetorical feature of OE poetry, notably frequent in Gl), and the all-embracing exclusiveness of the concessive general statement. There are grammarians, however, who claim that *both . . . and* and *whether . . . or* are notionally equal.[7]

Alternative concession takes many forms in the material, but whatever the form in detail, most of the examples present us with a pair of opposites. Often the opposing pairs occur more than once and seem to be stock phrases; for example, ' leof ne lað,' ' suð oððe norð,' ' god oððe yfel,' ' word oððe dæda ' are all recurrent; ' feor oððe neah ' and its variants like ' feorran oððe nean ' crop up in five poems—Gen, And, Jul, Wand, and Beo. Even more popular is the group 'ær oððe sið ' with its variants like ' sið ne ær,' ' ær ne sið ðan,' which occurs 16 times in the poetry (El, Chr, Gl, Rid, Jul, Menol, PrefDialogues, Beo). It may be supposed that such a cliché as this has not always full concessive feeling.

By far the most frequent form of the alternative concession, one which occurs throughout the material, is the verbless member consisting of a word and its antonym, the one preceding, the other following *oððe*.[8] The pattern is also twice used without the constituent parts being antonyms: ' mægen oððe merestream ' Ex 210, ' yldo oððe ærdeað ' Ex 540; in one instance (Gl 748) *oððe* contrasts two opposing but not antonymous full members with finite verbs. A slight variant of the pattern is to have *oððe* used twice, that is, correlatively; this variant occurs once : ' oþþe feor oþþe neah ' Jul 335.[9] A final variant is a series of any number of opposing, though not of course opposite, members separated by *oððe*; this occurs once in Soul 1 76 with *oððe* used three times separating four contrasting members, two with finite verbs and two without.[1]

The second most frequent form is a parallel construction to the foregoing, with *ne* instead of *oððe*. Separating antonymous pairs (like

---

7. Thus for instance Poutsma, op.cit.717.
8. On the MHG use of *oder* in alternative concessions, see Mensing, *Untersuchungen* 16ff.
9. So too in OE prose: ' oððe mid rihte oððe elles ' ASC E 1085.
1. In ASC A 597 we find *oððe* used four times with four members, the first *oððe* being an introductory correlative.

'freo ne þeowe' Gen 2747), *ne* occurs 11 times and in 9 poems. In one case the antonyms are finite verbs in the first person singular present:

Me nawþer deag,
secge ne swige.   (Chr 189)

The pattern is once used without the pair being antonyms: 'sceat ne scilling' Gen 2144. A variant form with correlative *ne . . . ne* is twice used with antonyms (Beo 510, El 571), and a series of opposing but not antonymous members occurs three times, twice with an initial correlative *ne*: Soul I 52, 57, Soul II 49. In the case of Soul I 57, *ne* is used six times to separate seven members.

To say that the pattern *swa . . . swa* occurs seven times in the poetry, though true, is to give a wrong impression of its currency, six of the examples being in successive lines of a passage beginning Chr 589, while the remaining one is in El 322. All these cases of correlative *swa* are with antonyms, though the antonymous members are not confined to single words as is usual with the previous patterns: 'swa lif swa deað' (Chr 596) is preceded by such pairs as 'swa þæt leohte leoht swa ða laþan niht' (Chr 592). All the seven cases however are of verbless members.

I have found only one certain example of *ge* used in an alternative concession, 'leofum ge laðum' Chr 846, though Burnham (p. 117) has found a number of examples of correlative *ge . . . ge* so used in the prose.

As we have seen, most of the alternative concessive members are verbless; those that are not contain verbs the mood of which is indeterminate; for example, Chr 189, quoted above.

Since the study of the form of these concessions is itself a study of their word order, we need say no more on this topic. A word is necessary however on the position of the concessive member in relation to the rest of the sentence. There are three main categories. In 27 cases the concessive member is placed medially in the member with which it is related, so that the verb of the main member follows the concessive group:

næfre he on aldordagum   ær ne siþðan
heardran hæle,   healðegnas fand!   (Beo 718)

This is the commonest order and it occurs in Gen, And, El, Chr, Gl, Jul, Wand, Wid, Rid, Bo, Menol, PrefDialogues, and Beo. The second type is only slightly different, the concession still being placed medially, but with the main verb preceding the concessive group; this occurs 16 times, in Gen, Soul I, Soul II, El, Chr, and Jud:

>   Ne hyrde ic sið ne ær
> on egstreame   idese lædan   (El 240)

Thirdly, the concessive member may come at the end:

>   næs þæra leoda ða
> ænig untrum   yldra ne gingra.   (ParPs 104/32)

This occurs 13 times, in Gen, Ex, Chr, Gl, Jud 1, ParPs, Bo, Exhort, and Prayer. Finally, if we accept the punctuation and interpretation of ASPR VI, 'Gode oððe yfle' in Sol 364 is a concessive group placed exceptionally in initial position.[2]

The position of the concessive member in the sentence is not apparently influenced by the particular form of the alternative concession.

There is little interest in the study of originals and parallel versions. Corresponding to the ParPs passage just quoted, the Latin reads simply, 'et non erat in tribubus eorum infirmus,' with no suggestion of concession. In Bo, two of the concessions (9/44, 10/24) are not to be found in the prose original, while the other (13/33) is an adaptation of the nonconcessive, inclusive group, 'ge monna ge neata,' found in the prose.

In summing up, the brevity and regular parallelism which Burnham found characterizing alternative concession in OE prose, characterize it equally in the verse. There are, however, marked differences between the prose and poetic constructions; *sam . . . sam* does not occur in the verse, and while the popular prose construction *swa . . . swa* is found a few times, the accompanying *swæðer* is absent from the verse; nor do we find the inverted *verb–subject* pairs (*beo he . . . beo he, wille we nelle we*) in the poetry. On the other hand, the construction with medial *oððe* or *ne*, which is most usual in the verse, seems relatively rare in OE prose. The alternative concession is usually placed medially in the member with which it is in concessive relation but in many cases it comes at the end and there is one uncertain example of it placed initially.

3. ZERO SUBORDINATOR

Formed in a similar way to the *beo he . . . beo he* type of alternative concession are concessions like 'Were he at death's door, I shouldn't go to see him.' The idiom is not infrequent in the earlier forms of the continental Germanic languages, and its use in the MHG *Nibel-*

---

2. On the other hand, Menner, for example, treats the two adjectives as nom.sg.neut. to be taken with *ðæt*, the last previous word, and not functioning as an alternative concession at all (*The Poetical Dialogues of Solomon and Saturn* [New York 1941]).

ungenlied and *Gudrun* has been analyzed in detail by Kuhlmann.³ Behagel illustrates the construction with several examples, among them the following quotation from Notker: 'heve sih ouh wig gagen mir, noh danne gedingo ich an in.'⁴ Burnham, while acknowledging that the idiom exists in OE, says that it appears only in the alternative concessive constructions, apart from "a few apparent exceptions" (p. 44). Unfortunately, she does not give any of these exceptions; it is possible that she had in mind the type, 'næfde he næfre swa mycel,' which though related is best classed with the other indefinite concessions.

In OE poetry the construction is to be found only once:

Wære ðu on wædle, sealdest me wilna geniht.

(Soul 1 144)

'Even though you were poor, you gave me . . .' The 'even' meaning seems to be inherent in the idiom, occurring so far as I know invariably in its MHG, ME, as in its NE forms. The notional kinship with the conditional relation also of course seems to be fundamental, as the form readily suggests, it being possible to express conditions with zero subordinator.

The mood in this one example is indeterminate. Burnham (p. 44) points out that the mood in all types of concession involving inversion in OE is invariably subjunctive, but as Kuhlmann and Behagel show (operibus cit.) indicative and subjunctive exist side by side in the MHG versions of the construction. Compare also: 'was I in a desert, I would find out wherewith in it to call forth my affections' (Sterne, *Sentimental Journey*).⁵

In conclusion, even with this meager material, we may object to Curme's observation (*Syntax* 338) that "This form of the concessive clause is unknown in Old English."

4. CONCESSIVE *gif*

Another construction with fundamental 'even' significance is the dependent concession introduced by (*even*) *if*, common in literary and colloquial forms alike of NE. It seems to be rare in OE, though in dealing with the prose material, Burnham (pp. 80-5) discusses a good number of passages,⁶ some concessive, some dubious, and some plainly

---

3. *Die Konzessivsätze* 11-13. Cf. too Mensing's study of *Parzival* in *Untersuchungen* 12.
4. *Deutsche Syntax* III.§1423.
5. For further examples of *was* in zero subordinations, see NED s.v. *be*, A.7.
6. Cf. also Mather, *Conditional Sentence* 21f.

nonconcessive. She finds *gif* translating (*et*)*si*, but since sometimes the translator obviously gives a conditional twist where the Latin was concessive, and since no examples have been found of *gif* rendering unambiguous Latin *quamvis, quamquam, licet* concessions, it puts the validity of concessive *gif* in a poor light.

In the poetry, four examples can be suggested, but only in the first can we be quite certain that *gif* is concessive:

> Gif þu him heodæg wuht   hearmes gespræce,
> he forgifð hit þeah,   gif wit him geongordom
> læstan willað.   (Gen 661)

The use of correlative *þeah* in the nondependent member here is interesting in view of OHG and MHG usage. Behaghel tells us that *ob* was used to introduce a dependent concession when a clarifying particle was also present. The following example is from Otfrid: ' ob ih iz sagen iu, ir ni giloubet thoh bi thiu.' Gradually, he says, *ob* was joined by such elements as *gleich* to serve this clarifying purpose.[7] The same phenomenon of *gif* . . . *þeah* occurs in some of Burnham's examples from the prose, but even when this is translating a clearly concessive Latin construction, she inclines to interpret the OE as being of a double function, " first as a condition: ' take the case when,' " and secondly, " the writer views it also as a concession " and therefore he " adds an adversative " (p. 82).[8]

The second example is:

> næfre meldade   monna ængum
> gif me ordstæpe   egle wæron.   (Rid 72/17)

Mackie (*Exeter Book* 211) is in support of a concessive interpretation here: '(I) never made complaint to any man, even if the stabs of the goad were painful to me.' The absence of a correlative adversative in the nondependent member makes it difficult to be dogmatic, but *gif* taken conditionally would be tantamount to requiring an introductory ' provided that,' which is well-nigh absurd.

Finally, we have two examples in Charm 4, the one having four dependent *gif*-members, the other three; since editors have differed as to which are the related nondependent members, the whole context is given:

> Gif her inne sy   *isernes dæl,
> hægtessan geweorc,   hit sceal gemyltan.

---

7. *Deutsche Syntax* III.§1424 B. On MHG concessive *ob*, see also Mensing, *Untersuchungen* 69f.

8. Contrast Lerch's attitude to ' das bedingte Konzessivverhältnis,' *Hist.franz.Synt.* I.260–9.

> Gif ðu wære on fell scoten   oððe wære on flæsc scoten
> oððe wære on blod scoten
> oððe wære on lið scoten,   næfre ne sy ðin lif atæsed;
> gif hit wære esa gescot   oððe hit wære ylfa gescot
> oððe hit wære hægtessan gescot,   nu ic wille ðin helpan.
>   *MS: isenes   (Charm 4/18)

In the rest of the charm, it is not the practice to make major syntactical breaks in the middle of the line, and so it would seem that dependent and nondependent members are related in the way indicated by the punctuation in ASPR.[9]

While it is clear that the *gif*-member in l. 18 is conditional, it seems likely that the sequence in 20–2 should be interpreted as concessive, 'even if' or 'whether you were ... or ...' But no doubt these *gif*-members can be regarded as conditional also, postulating individual cases in which the patient need have no cause for worry; Dobbie (ASPR vi.213) refers to this and the subsequent series in 23f. as 'hypothetical condition.' At first sight, these latter *gif*-members strike one quite forcibly as concessive, 'no matter if,' 'even if,' the whole being a generalizing challenge that help is assured whatever the origin of the evil; yet in 25f. ('Þis ðe to bote esa gescotes ...') the three origins are treated as individual cases and it is expressly stated that 'this is a remedy' for all three.

The mood of the verbs in these examples is indeterminate or subjunctive ('hit wære' three times), but in the prose examples of *gif* used in a possibly concessive function, there are both determinate indicative and subjunctive forms of the verb, so that mood would not in any case be a helpful criterion in our examples. Moreover, since the material ends here, with no Latin sources and no parallel versions of the poetic examples, we can only conclude that *gif* could be used concessively in OE but that it is very rare. It is relevant to note, indeed, that the most reliable of the poetic examples comes from Gen B, the part of the poem originating in an OS form. By the early ME period, however, we can be sure that concessive *gif* was well established, since in his study of the *Layamon* manuscripts, Bøgholm has found *gif* in one manuscript corresponding several times to *þeah* in another,[1] both elements sharing conditional and concessive functions.

---

9. For a summary of other views, see Grein-Wülker, *Bibliothek* 1.318.
1. *The Layamon Texts* 60f.

5. INDEFINITE CONCESSIONS

The indefinite concession is like the alternative in that it seeks to challenge any attempt to deny the validity of the member to which it is related. But whereas the alternative type does this by specifying such wide limits as make denial impossible, the indefinite does it in a generalizing challenge which says that there are no limits. As Schücking says in connection with Beo 1394: " Der sprechende bezeichnet hier das Eintreten eines Ereignisses nicht nur durch die Einräumung als gleichgiltig, sondern fordert sogar auf, dasselbe herbeizuführen und betont, dass trotzdem die Giltigkeit des 2. Satzes bestehen bleibt." [2] In effect, there is little to choose between the degree of exclusiveness expressed by these two concessive constructions:

> Brother or not, I would unmask him.
> Whoever he were, I would unmask him.

But frequently they are not as interchangeable as they appear here. In the face of ' Rain or fine, I'm going,' an indefinite concession like ' Whatever the weather does . . .' is not only verbose and clumsy but lacks the essential preciseness of the former construction. One cannot replace the alternative by an indefinite concession in the following example: ' and later on you won't even care whether he comes or not ' (Jenny); nor in the next can the indefinite concession be replaced by an alternative one: ' Whatever I've done, I'll put right ' (Jenny).

Indefinite concessive constructions in NE have been studied in detail (and often with historical data) by Curme, Jespersen, and Poutsma, while certain aspects have been discussed by Charleston, Sonnenschein, and Stoffel. For the ME period, one should draw attention to the general syntactical studies of C. S. Baldwin,[3] Bøgholm, and Mossé. For the OE period, the only detailed study is Burnham's excellent chapter (pp. 51–65), but Behre, Einenkel, Ericson, Glunz, Schücking, and Trnka have all made contributions.[4]

An outline of the notional range of the indefinite concession will serve to explain the classification adopted below. Expressed with various forms of the indefinite relative pronoun, we have the concession applied to *persons*: ' Whoe'er he be, you may not be let in ' (*I Henry VI* 1.iii.7); likewise, to *things*: ' But whateuer he had in þou3t, Mis-

---

2. *Grundzüge der Satzverknüpfung* §15.
3. *The Inflections and Syntax of the Morte d'Arthur of Sir Thomas Malory* (Boston 1894).
4. On indefinite concessions in MHG with *swer* (OHG *sô hwer sôso*), *swenne* (*sô hwanne sô*), *swie* (*sô wio sô*), see Mensing, *Untersuchungen* 39f., 46f., 47f. respectively.

likyng chere had he nouȝt' (*Cursor Mundi* 11/143). The concession is applied to the *temporal* relation: ' if his fitness speaks, mine is ready; now or whensoever, provided I be so able as now' (*Hamlet* v.ii.210). Similarly, we have indefinite *local* concessions: ' Would I were with him, wheresome'er he is, either in heaven or in hell' (*Henry V* II.iii.7). Finally, various constructions of indefinite *degree* give us relationships like the following: ' Houeuer antecrist glauer, he letteþ not god do his wille' (Wyclif, *Works* 330).

Of these five types of relationship, four are represented in the present material, there being no indefinite temporal concession, and to judge from Burnham's study this type is rare also in OE prose. This is not to say that indefinite temporal members themselves do not exist: there are many examples of *þonne, hwonne* (*hwænne*) in such functions. For instance:

Þonne on hinderling hweorfað mine
feondas fæcne, ðonne ic me freoðu to ðe
wordum wilnige   (ParPs 55/8)

The second *þonne* means *whenever* (Latin ' in quacumque die,' VespPs ' on swehwelcum dege '), but that does not make it concessive. One of the difficulties in handling this material is deciding when the examples are concessive and when they are simply indefinite, for, as Burnham notes, the form of the concessive type " agrees closely with that of certain mere general permissions or exhortations " (p. 51). But there is a school of thought which denies that this distinction exists. Glunz argues that the sentence ' se mon, se þe his gewealdes monnan ofslea, swelte se deaðe' (Laws 58.13) means ' all men who kill must die' which in turn is equivalent to a generalizing challenge, ' no matter what men they are who kill, they must die.' " Der Satz ist also konzessiv und der verallgemeinernde Konjunktiv derselbe wie in Konzessivsätzen." Similarly, in the sentence, ' eal ðæt flæsc þæt wildeor læfen, ne eten ge þæt, ac sellað hit hundum' (Laws 62.39), we have indefinite concession. Under the same head, says Glunz, are to be reckoned relative clauses where the antecedent is a positive adjective: ' beoð simle gearwe . . . to forgifonne ælcum (men), ðara þe eow . . . bidde' (*Cura Past.* 172.8); or where it is a superlative: ' Cristes rod . . . selest sigebeacna þara þe . . . ahafen wurde' (El 972); or where it is a determining negative: ' ne wæs on ða tid ænig bisceop, ðara ðe rihtlice gehalgod wære' (Bede 560.28).[5]

Poutsma takes up a less extreme position than Glunz. He points out that the sentence, ' I will follow you wherever you go,' can be interpreted as ' I will follow you to any place you may go to ' (indefinite

---

5. *Verwendung des Konjunktivs* 60–5.

relative), or 'I will follow you, whatever may be the place you go to' (indefinite concession). It depends, he says, on whether "the uncertainty which attaches to them concerns the action or state denoted by the predicate or the person or thing indicated by the pronoun to which these words are appended." Nevertheless, he goes on to give examples of concession which seem very dubious: 'Let whoso thinketh he standeth, take good heed lest he fall,' 'Whatever harm was in some of them was not there for me,' 'I think whoever has carried this story to you might have been better occupied.'[6]

The distinction must be drawn, it seems to me, between the generalizing, inclusive, indefinite meaning on the one hand, and, on the other, the challenging defiance the same constructions can assume in concessive function. The distinction is a simple matter to make when the dependent and nondependent members have different subjects, compare for example the following sentences:

> Whoever comes will find a welcome.
> Whoever comes, I shan't open the door.

When the subject of both members is the same, however, we have more difficulty:

> Whoever eats it will enjoy it.
> This cake is so good that whoever eats it will enjoy it.

Only the fuller context in the latter case is able to show us that the indefinite construction is meant to be concessive. In some respects we may say, despite Glunz, that when the idea of totality ('all who') is uppermost we have no concession, but when the idea of exclusiveness, individuality ('no matter who') is uppermost we have concession. In presenting the OE material, the examples cited are only those that can be reckoned as certainly concessive from the context, and it must be remembered, particularly in the case of the 'whoever' and 'whatever' types, that the concessive examples given are by far outnumbered by those about which certainty has not seemed possible.

The use of *swa* with the indefinite relatives is exhaustively studied by Ericson,[7] but it is to be noted that even in combination with *swa* (in modern form a fair guide to concessive feeling today), the indefinite pronouns are sometimes used nonconcessively.

The easiest kind of indefinite concession to identify is the 'challenge' type. The study of the 'permissive' subjunctive in this construction

---

6. *Grammar* II.1217.
7. 'Use of Old English *swa* in Negative Clauses'; cf. also Olaf Johnsen, 'Indefinite Relatives'; on the modern derivatives of *swa*, see Stoffel, *Intensives and Downtoners*, and Jespersen, *Mod.Engl.Gr.*, especially III.9.41ff.

has been admirably conducted by Behre,[8] both in general terms and with specific attention to OE usage; the challenge function of the verb is also underlined by Charleston,[9] Trnka,[1] and Jespersen, who suggests a coalescence in function as well as in form of subjunctive, imperative, and infinitive in the modern usage of the 'come what may' type.[2]

We have already noticed (IV.2) that there are forms of the concessive relation which some grammarians prefer to class with condition. The indefinite constructions are commonly so interpreted. Schücking (*Satzverknüpfung* §15a) takes his predecessor Nader to task for calling the example of 'go where he will' in Beo 1394 'conditional' instead of 'concessive.' Sonnenschein groups concessive examples like 'Do what you may' with conditional ones like 'Bouge, je te tue,' apparently without feeling that there is any incongruity.[3] Similarly, the able syntactician Fernand Mossé, turning to the conditional relation after dealing with concession, classes under 'Subordonnées Conditionnelles' the following examples of 'l'inversion conditionnelle . . . avec subordonnant zéro': 'were it never so unprevable,' 'Ne sunge ich hom never so longe,' along with purely conditional examples of the inversion construction.[4] As with the double function of *if* (for condition and 'even' concession), the parallel twin functions of the inversion construction show that speakers recognize the notional closeness of the two relationships; note in this connection Einenkel's words: "Diese Frageform des Bedingungssatzes ist nun, *ob auf ihn übertragen oder nicht*, auch am Konzessivsatze zu beobachten."[5]

6. INDEFINITE CONCESSIONS OF DEGREE

We begin with the type of indefinite concession of which there are most examples in our material. The type shows considerable variety of pattern, but basically it is like the modern parallel in consisting of an adjective or adverb together with a particle indicating the indefinite extent of the quality in question. There seem to be some 15 examples (including one which is of exceptional pattern and about which there has been controversy) in OE poetry. They are distributed as follows:

---

8. *Subjunctive in Old English Poetry*, especially pp. 11, 45ff.
9. *Studies on the Syntax of the English Verb* 146.
1. *Syntaktická Charakteristika* 101-2.
2. *Mod.Engl.Gr.* v.12.61f.
3. *Soul of Grammar* §119.
4. *Moyen-Anglais* §§158, 175.
5. *Geschichte* II.43 (italics mine).

Gen (B) 1, Dan 1, ChrSat 1, Soul 1 1, Gl 1, Jul 2, Seaf 1, Order 1, Jud 1 1, Hell 1, Sol 2, Beo 2. For example:

>Næfre mon þæs hlude   horn aþyteð
>ne byman ablaweþ,   þæt ne sy seo beorhte stefn
>ofer ealne middangeard   monnum hludre   (Jud 1 109)
>
>þeah me . . .
>hete heofones god . . .
>on flod faran,   nære he firnum þæs deop,
>merestream þæs micel,   þæt his o min mod getweode,
>ac ic to þam grunde genge   (Gen 830)

With the latter compare 'ne him to ne dorste sciphere on sæ. ne landfyrd. ne eodon hi swa feor up' (ASC E 1001), 'no libbe he swa longe' (*Layamon* 2207), 'Ne beo þe song neuer so murie' (*Owl & Night.* 345).

Five times we have the concessive member introduced by *næfre* followed by the subject, the indefinite degree, and finally the verb: Jul 55, 176, Sol 68, 146, Jud 1 109 (quoted above). A variant of this occurs in Beo 967 and possibly also 1508, using *no* instead of *næfre*:

>ic hine ne mihte,   þa Metod nolde,
>ganges getwæman,   no ic him þæs georne ætfealh,
>feorhgeniðlan   (Beo 967)[6]

There is another variant in Soul 1 97:

>. . . ne bið nan na to þæs lytel lið   on fime aweaxen,
>þæt ðu ne scyle . . .

In four examples the concessive member is introduced by a negated form of the verb, followed by the subject and then the indefinite degree: Gen 830 (quoted above), ChrSat 515, Seaf 39, Hell 64. In a further case, the member begins with the expression of degree:

>No þæs fela Daniel   to his drihtne gespræc
>soðra worda   ðurh snytro cræft,
>þæt þæs a se rica   reccan wolde   (Dan 593)

Gl 865 is irregular, combining some features of all the foregoing types:

>Nænig monna wæs
>of þam sigetudre   siþþan æfre
>godes willan þæs georn

---

6. On the interpretation of this as concessive, see Kock, Anglia xliii.304, xlvi.83f., and Klaeber's note (ed., p. 167); one cannot so easily follow Kock in reckoning 'no þon lange' in Beo 2419 a further example, 'however long.'

The following example is exceptional in pattern and somewhat dubious:

> Ic þe lungre sceal
> meotudes mægensped   maran gesecgan,
> þonne þu hygecræftig   in hreþre mæge
> mode gegripan.   Is *þin meaht forswiþ.
> Thus the MS; ASPR III emends to *sin*.   (Order 23)

In ASPR III.309 other examples are given of the error *þ* for *s* in OE manuscripts to justify the editors' emendation here. Other editors, however, keep the manuscript reading, and Mackie (*Exeter Book* 48) interprets the member as concessive and thus parallel to the undoubted concessive function of *hygecræftig* in the previous line: 'however great your ability.' Accepting this interpretation is not made easier by the fact that this would be the only degree concession in OE poetry formed without *þæs*.

It will be seen that there is room for much debate in the interpretation of degree concessions in OE poetry. This is especially so since the *þæs* idiom is long since dead and the whole sentence has to be re-formed to demonstrate the concessive relation. It may indeed be that degree concession should be interpreted rather more widely than has been done here, to include other instances of *þæs* (such as that in Jul 510), and indefinite degree expressions which appear in question form:

> Hwylc is þæs mihtig   ofer middangeard,
> þæt he þe alyse   of leoðubendum,
> manna cynnes,   ofer mine est?   (And 1372)

This would seem, however, to be interpreting the logical implication of a grammatical expression rather than analyzing the grammatical expression of a particular relationship.

The only exception, then, to the use of *þæs* in the degree concessions of the poetry is the dubious use of the intensifier *for-* in Order 23. We do not find *swa*, although this seems to be the usual particle in the prose; indeed, to judge from Burnham's remarks (pp. 59–61), *swa* is the only element in prose usage.

A most regular feature of these concessions is the negative verb; again, the only exception is the irregular construction of Order 23. The negation is usually expressed strongly: *næfre*, *nænig* . . . *æfre*, *no*, *nære* . . . *firnum*.

The position of the concessive member in relation to the rest of the sentence is of structural importance. For the most part, the concessive member precedes the member to which it is related, and in these cases the *þæs* correlates with a *þæt* which introduces the second and related member.[7] This structure seems not to be found in the prose. In the remaining cases, the concessive member comes second and is much more loosely connected to the member with which it is in concessive relation; indeed, there is little to indicate that these concessive members containing þæs (corresponding to swa in prose) involve grammatical dependence at all:

>   Mæg simle se godes cwide   gumena gehwylcum
>   ealra feonda gehwane   fleondne gebrengan
>   ðurh mannes muð,   manfulra heap
>   sweartne geswencan,   næfre hie ðæs syllice
>   bleoum bregdað.   (Sol 146)

The last observation that we need make concerning pattern and arrangement is that parallel concessive members as poetical variations appear on two occasions (Gen 830, Hell 64), in neither case with duplication of the verb, although the apparent ellipsis of the second verb in one case may be merely due to the defective manuscript:

>   ne bið he no þæs nearwe   under niðloc(. . .
>   . . .) þæs bitre gebunden   under bealuclommum,
>   þæt he þy yð ne mæge   ellen habban   (Hell 64)

Burnham's examples from the prose (p. 59f.) all show subjunctive mood in the dependent member, except for a couple of indeterminate examples. The poetic material is startingly different; only one indefinite concessive member has a subjunctive verb (Gen 830), and the rest have indicative verbs, there being no indeterminate forms. Thus the position of the concessive member in the sentence has no effect on the mood of the concessive verb; but it has a marked effect on the mood of the verb in the related member. When the concessive member follows (that is, the 'loose' structure already mentioned), the verb of the preceding member is indicative in five cases and for the rest is indeterminate. But when the concessive member precedes, whether its verb is subjunctive (Gen 830) or not, the verb of the following member, introduced by þæt, is subjunctive or—in a few cases—indeterminate.

There are no Latin or OE sources to consider in our material, and no parallel texts.

To sum up, while the indefinite concession of degree is formed in the prose by constructions with swa, the verb being in the subjunctive, in the poetry it is formed by constructions with þæs, the verb usually being in the indicative. The þæs-member for the most part takes initial position and is strongly negative, the member with which it

---

[7]. This feature reminds us of the notional closeness of the present type of concession to *result*.

is in concessive relation being introduced by a correlative and having its verb in the subjunctive. This order and construction seem not to occur in the prose. The remaining concessions in the poetry, mostly negative, follow the member to which they are—more loosely—related; in this type neither member has a subjunctive verb.

7. INDEFINITE RELATIVE CONCESSIONS: 'WHOEVER'

These concessions are rare in the poetry and, outside certain limits, in the prose also, where they "are found chiefly in the Laws and Charters; other instances are scattered" (Burnham, p. 52). This is not to say that indefinite relative constructions in general are rare, or that if we were to interpret 'concession' with the freedom of Glunz and Poutsma our results would be so meager. The situation is the same in poetry and prose in this respect too, and Burnham complains that it is "sometimes difficult ... to decide whether or not a given indefinite clause has a concessive coloring" (p. 53). For instance in the Junius MS there are some 19 indefinite relative constructions, but only one of them can be reckoned certainly concessive. Yet many of the excluded examples might well be so interpreted if we were prepared to look upon the generalization as conveying a 'no matter who' indifference:

> Forþon se bið eadig   se ðe æfre wile
> man oferhycgen,   meotode cweman,
> synne adwæscan. (ChrSat 303)

But this would make the analysis very subjective, and so in deciding between concessive and nonconcessive it has seemed better to risk excluding the former rather than to include the latter.

There are only seven examples in OE poetry which we can be sure are concessive; all are preceded by the members to which they are syntactically related and are distributed as follows: Ex 1, Bo 3, Beo 3. They are all of the 'challenge' type:

> Gehyre se ðe wille! (Ex 7)
> Sinc eaðe mæg,
> gold on *grund(e)   gumcynnes gehwone
> oferhigian,   hyde se ðe wylle!
> *MS defective at edge. (Beo 2764)

This challenge pattern is not, however, inherently concessive. In Rid, for example, we several times find the formula used nonconcessively:

DEPENDENT CONCESSIONS WITHOUT þeah IV.8

      Secge se þe cunne,
wisfæstra hwylc, hwæt seo wiht sy.   (Rid 67/15)

Compare also, 'Ræde, se þe wille' Rid 59/15, 'Hliste se þe wille' Bo Proem 10.

It is to be noted that six of the seven challenges have 'se þe wille' as the relative member; the exception (Beo 1387) has 'se þe mote.' Trnka points out that the present subjunctive has concessive significance in relative sentences containing *willan*,[8] but such nonconcessive examples as 'Ræde, se þe wille' show that this, while generally true, is not necessarily always so. Nor must the verb which has the relative member as its subject necessarily be in the subjunctive. Two of the three examples from Bo have the indicative, though this seems to be unparalleled in Burnham's material and is rare enough in the later language:[9]

  Eala, þæt is hefig dysig, hygeð ymbe se ðe wile
                 (Bo 19/1)
    Is ðæt micel gecynd
þines goodes, þencð ymb se ðe wile (Bo 20/26)

As for the mood of the verb in the relative member, there is no evidence of the indicative, but most of the recorded forms are indeterminate.

There are no Latin sources to be considered, and the three challenge concessions in Bo are absent from the OE prose source.

8. INDEFINITE RELATIVE CONCESSIONS: 'WHICH-, WHATEVER'

Again we must begin with the caveat that many indefinite constructions are left out of account because they are not convincingly concessive. Those that are without doubt concessive are rare, amounting only to 10, distributed as follows: Gen (B) 2, Jul 1, Wand 1, Prec 1, Partridge 1, ParPs 2, Exhort 1, Beo 1. In view of the small number, the variety of pattern is notable. The challenge type appears four times:

      Ic to soþe wat
þæt biþ in eorle indryhten þeaw,
þæt he his ferðlocan fæste binde,
*healde his hordcofan, hycge swa he wille.
  *MS: healdne   (Wand 11)

---

8. *Syntaktická Charakteristika* 101.
9. See Burnham, pp. 51–3, Jespersen, *Mod.Engl.Gr.* v.12.61, Poutsma, *Grammar* I.II.714. Wilmanns, *Deutsche Grammatik* III.I.261, reckoned the subjunctive fundamental in this type of concession in Gmc, but cf. Behaghel, *Deutsche Syntax* III.§1423.

So too, Prec 23, ParPs 93/7, Exhort 16. But even within the challenge type there is variety; one example has both verbs in the preterite: 'dyde swa he wolde' ParPs 93/7; two of the four do not use *willan* in the indefinite member (*mæge* Prec 23, *wyrce* Exhort 16). Indeed, Exhort 16 does not use *swa* but has a substantive *þæt*-member as object to an imperative—not a subjunctive—governing verb; furthermore, in this example the whole concession precedes the syntactically related member and so is different from the other challenge constructions in this and the previous section:

> Wyrc þæt þu wyrce,   word oððe dæda,
> hafa metodes ege   on gemang . . .

It may have been the rarity of this type that caused Grein to analyze the concessive member here incorrectly as "the protasis of a conditional sentence."[1] Apart however from the use of the imperative (natural enough in the second person singular), this type with the double use of one verb and with *þæt* for *swa* is amply paralleled in Burnham's material; the prose Bo has 'wyrce . . . ðæt he wyrce' 112/19, and other examples are given by Burnham, pp. 52–3.

Secondly, we may group together the examples in which a noun is made the center of an indefinite concession; this occurs four times. In one case the indefinite construction is *swa hwilc–substantive–swa*, the verb being indicative:

> In swa hwylce tiid   swa ge mid treowe to me
> on hyge hweorfað   (Partridge 5)

In ParPs 137/4, the construction is similar but lacks a second *swa*, and the verb is indeterminate, while Gen 551, where the verb is indicative, has no initial *swa*. In a further example, *hwæðer* replaces *hwilc*, the verb being subjunctive:

>   ond siþðan witig God
> on swa hwæþere hond   halig Dryhten
> mærðo deme,   swa him gemet þince.   (Beo 685)

Thirdly, we have *swa hwæt swa*, which occurs concessively once, the verb being indicative: 'Swa hwæt swa wit her morðres þoliað, hit is . . . forgolden' Gen 755.

Finally, there is the following example with the subjunctive which is not paralleled in the poetry and only fairly remotely in the prose (Burnham, pp. 59–60):

> Dem þu hi to deaþe . . .
> swa to life læt,   swa þe leofre sy.   (Jul 87)

'Condemn her to death, or let her live, whichever you prefer.'

---

1. See ASPR vi.183; note also what has been said above on interpreting indefinite concessions as conditional constructions (iv.5).

There is little to note about sources or other comparative material. In ParPs, the most remarkable point is the apparent dislike of the English translator for the Latin indefinite constructions; time and again we find the OE version has nothing to correspond to these Latin forms. For example, in ParPs 101/2 in the space of three lines the translator avoids the Latin 'in quacumque die' twice and makes no attempt even to replace it. On the other hand, the concessive example, 'Swa hwylce daga' 137/4, renders the Latin 'in quacumque die,' and in 93/7 the OE translator inserts an indefinite challenge concession where there is nothing to correspond in the Latin.

To sum up, there are two main constructions for this type of concession in OE, the challenge and the *swa* (*hwilc*) . . . *swa* pattern, both showing some variety. The former uses the subjunctive, the latter usually the indicative but the subjunctive is also found.

9. INDEFINITE CONCESSIONS OF PLACE

These concessions are even rarer than the indefinite types already examined. There are only four convincing examples: Gen 1 (not in Gen B), Ex 1, And 1, Beo 1. There are two types of construction. First, there is the indefinite *þær*-member which occurs three times, the verb being in the subjunctive in each case; thus:

  Wuna mid usic and þe wic geceos
  on þissum lande þær þe leofost sie (Gen 2723)

So too, Ex 271, And 223. The subjunctive in these examples seems significant, since when we find nonconcessive *þær*-members used indefinitely they have the indicative; for example:

      Wast nu þe gearwor
 þæt ic eaðe mæg anra gehwylcne
 fremman ond fyrþran freonda minra
 on landa gehwylc, þær me leofost bið. (And 932)

Secondly, we have the challenge construction used once:

  Ic hit þe gehate: no he on helm losaþ,
  ne on foldan fæþm . . .
      . . . ga þær he wille! (Beo 1392)

Burnham (p. 56f.) gives several examples of the latter construction, but makes no reference to the indefinite *þær*-member used concessively.

Apart from these four concessions there are the usual dubious cases where indefinite constructions are used in a generalizing and nonconcessive way. We have no sources or parallel texts to consider.

10. CONCESSIVE-EQUIVALENT CONSTRUCTIONS

In notional research along the lines laid down by Brunot, one does not stop at autonomous means of relational expression.[2] We have already seen that certain temporal elements—*gyt*, *þonne*, and others—can have a concessive function while they also retain their temporal significance. The case is different with *ac*, for example, which is used in other functions *as well as* in concession; this does not make it a 'concessive-equivalent' in the sense in which I intend the term, since each of its functions excludes the others. Nor has the expression anything to do with elements and constructions merely coming to have an extended use beyond an earlier one. Thus in NE, *while* has both temporal and concessive function, the latter being derivative, but it is not a 'concessive equivalent' because when it is concessive it is not normally temporal as well; compare:

> While there is no war, we must believe in peace.
> While there is no war, we are hardly in a true peace.

The former use of *while* is wholly temporal, the latter wholly concessive and not concessive-equivalent. Similarly: 'And where thou now exact'st the penalty . . . Thou wilt . . . Forgive a moiety of the principal' (*Merchant* IV.i.22). The *where*-member here has no local sense and is therefore not a concessive-equivalent construction.

On the other hand, in the following example the *when*-member retains its temporal function but combines with it a concessive function; it is thus a case of *when* as a concessive-equivalent element: 'We sometimes look for praise when we've done nothing to deserve it.' So too, the relative clause in the following example is a concessive-equivalent member:

> perhaps in this emergency you will bear with their antiquity and the scent of lavender, which also, I fear, is not of the mode today.   (Harold Brighouse, *Alison's Island*)

The next example, also of a relative member used concessively, is supplied by Curme (*Syntax* 338): 'Many boys who have had few advantages by birth work their way to fame.'

Existing as it does in many languages, the phenomenon has been noticed by scholars from time to time. In 1892 Kellner drew attention to "Adverbial Clauses relating to Manner and Degree" which are

---

2. *La Pensée et la langue.* Cf. the important contribution to this field made by Small, PMLA li.1–7.

used also " in a concessive sense." [3] Dubislav made a special collection of ME examples; for instance: 'Ioseph hem knew als he let he knew hem nogt' (*Gen and Ex* 2167); [4] one is of particular interest: 'And deme that hii don ille, there I do wel worse' (*Piers Plowman* 63/104). As there is no local sense in *there*, it might be thought that this is autonomously concessive; but in fact *there* is used temporally and this sense co-exists with the concessive, thus making it concessive-equivalent. For the NE period, we have the notes on intonation and function made by Schubiger,[5] and the brilliant analysis of the phenomenon in Curme's *Syntax*.[6]

In relation to the OE constructions, we are fortunate in having Burnham's long chapter (pp. 66–94) devoted to the problem of the equivalent clauses. She puts her finger on the essential point when she says (p. 66) that "Such clauses often indicate an attempt to say or suggest two things at once—the concessive idea superadded to some other."

It has already been said that the definite establishment and recognition of the concessive relation is not always an easy matter, even when we are dealing with autonomous concessive constructions. It may therefore be imagined how much more this is so when we are dealing with the explicit expressions of other relationships and are looking only for an underlying and subsidiary concessive relation. As Burnham says, "the concessive element may be more or less distinct in a given case, and classifications become debatable" (p. 66). In every concessive-equivalent construction now to be described, many examples were found in which the concessive feeling was not sufficiently obvious or convincing for them to be included in the statistics. The only examples counted in this as in other sections of this study are those of which we can feel reasonably certain.

11. CONCESSIVE-EQUIVALENT RELATIVE MEMBERS

By far the most frequent concessive-equivalent construction in OE prose and poetry alike is the ordinary relative clause. Its validity as a concessive expression is established beyond question over and over

---

3. *Historical Outlines* §§127–8.
4. 'Studien,' *Anglia* xl.262–321. Several of his examples, however, are incorrectly analyzed.
5. *Role of Intonation*, especially p. 29f.
6. It should be noted that when Onions (*Advanced English Syntax* §58b) uses the term 'equivalents,' he is not using the term in our sense but means rather 'abridgments' of concessive clauses.

again. We need pause to give only one example; in the poetic Bo we have a dependent member formed with *þeah* and the subjunctive, 'ðeah ðu ... geta ... hæbbe' (24/46), where in the original prose the same relation is rendered by a relative member with the indicative: 'þe ðu ... geot ... hafst.'

Relative members with concessive function occur in OE verse 82 times (not counting those that seem doubtful), distributed as follows: Gen 4 (2 in Gen B), Ex 1, Dan 3, ChrSat 3, And 4, Soul I 2, El 11, Chr 10, Gl 4, Ph 1, Jul 2, Prec 1, Soul II 3, Deor 1, Rid 4, Resig 1, Hell 1, ParPs 6, Bo 7, Maldon 5, Exhort 1, Beo 5, Jud 2. For example:

       Þæt me is sorga mæst,
 þæt Adam sceal, þe wæs of eorðan geworht,
 minne stronglican stol behealdan   (Gen 364)

       ond þa weregan neat,
 þe man daga gehwam drifeð ond þirsceð,
 ongitaþ hira goddend   (El 357)

       on flet gæð,
 morðres *gylpeð, ond þone maðþum byreð,
 þone þe ðu mid rihte rædan sceoldest.
 *MS (Thork.B): gylped   (Beo 2054)

Elliptical concessions are found with this as they are with other constructions; in the following example, the real concession is not 'although I had hurt none, I lay in the grave,' which is nonsense, but rather 'although I had done no hurt, I was put to death and laid in the earth':

 Læg min flæschoma in foldan bigrafen,
 niþre gehyded, se ðe nængum scod,
 in byrgenne   (Chr 1465)

In one case the concessive relative clause depends on an emendation; the manuscript reads:

 Ðu þæt gehatest þæt ðu ham on hus
 gegan wille, eart ðe godes yrming. (Gl 271)

For *hus* of course editors read *us*, but the solution to the problem of the last half-line is not so obvious. Thorpe suggested *eart ðu*, thus making the member concessive without relating element; ASPR III.57 reads *ðe eart*, transposing without further emendation, but in the notes (p. 263) the editors suggest that perhaps we ought to read *ðeah* for *ðe*. There is little to choose between these three possibilities, each giving well-established concessive constructions; I accept the version *ðe eart* printed in ASPR (thus making the member a concessive-equivalent relative clause), though with some reluctance since this kind of transposition is not the commonest of scribal errors.

By virtue of its indicating the pluperfect tense, *ær* frequently appears in these concessions, reinforcing and pointing the relationship. " Clauses of this sort, though without formal adversatives, are often contrasted with the principal clause through the use of *ær* and other particles " (Burnham, p. 71), and in our material *ær* is so used in nearly half of the examples. It appears in Gen, Ex, Dan, ChrSat, And, El, Chr, Ph, Soul II, Deor, Rid, ParPs, Bo, Maldon, Exhort, Beo, and Jud. For instance:

> . . . ðu, sarum forsoht,   wiðsæcest fæste
> þone ahangnan cyning,   þam ðu hyrdest ær.   (El 932)

It sometimes appears in the comparative form (for example, Beo 809); sometimes it is joined by *lange* in the same function (Soul I 122, II 117, Hell 53, Bo 13/37, 22/16, El 600); in Bo 22/5 we have *sume hwile . . . æror*, in Jud 212 *hwile ær*, and there are other similar groupings; it is correlated with *nu* in the nondependent member of ParPs 117/21. But the frequency of *ær* in these relative members does not mean that its occurrence is a sure pointer to the concessive function; *ær* also occurs in nonconcessive relative members. For example:

> þa wearð yrre god
> and þam werode wrað   þe he ær wurðode
> wlite and wuldre.   (Gen 34)

The concessive function of relative clauses is pointed by other elements than *ær*, though in not nearly such large numbers. In And 578, Jul 205, Rid 15/27, Jud 155, we have *lange*, in Bo 20/263 *þrage nu . . . hwyle*, in ParPs 75/5 *hwilon*; in El 297 and Maldon 186 we have *oft*, in Bo 22/13 *oftost nu*, in Maldon 198 *eft*, Bo 2/10 *æfre*, Soul I 57 *iu*, El 357 *daga gehwam*, El 813 *nalles feam siðum*. We find *gen* used as the reinforcing element twice (El 1079, 1089); compare also Bo 24/46, where the prose original has a relative clause reinforced by *geot* as we have seen above. It may also be that the use of *eall*[7] in the concessive relative member of ParPs 105/27 is significant:

> agutan blod swylce   bearna feala,
> þa unscyldige   ealle wærun

This leaves only about a third of the concessive relative clauses which appear without any reinforcing element.

Occasionally we have parallel relative members subordinated to a single nondependent member; in El 297 and Chr 1484 we have two

---

7. See also below IV.23.

such members parallel; in ParPs 105/18 we have four, from two of which the verb is absent by ellipsis. These are the only occasions on which we find verbless relative members used concessively. The example from ParPs is as follows:

>   Godes hi forgeaton,   þe hi of gramra ær
>   feonda folmum   frecne generede,
>   þe on Egyptum   æðele *wundur
>   and on Chananea   cymu worhte
>   and recene wundur   on þam readan sæ
>   MS: wundar   (ParPs 105/18)

Each occurrence of parallel concessive relative members has been counted only as a single concession for statistical purposes.

The range of word order in these concessive members is the same as in nonconcessive relative members. We thus have nothing to add to the data supplied by Fourquet, *L'Ordre des éléments* 69f., 108f., 184f.

In the majority of cases, the concessive member follows the nondependent member to which it is related. This can be seen in most of the examples already quoted. There are, however, eight examples of the concessive member placed medially in the nondependent member, often preceded only by the antecedent of the relative; these are Gen 364, El 907, Chr 937, 1465, 1480, 1484, ParPs 117/21, and Beo 2864. The proportion in Chr seems especially noteworthy. A typical example of this order is the following:

>   Þone sylfan stan   þe hine swyðe ær
>   wyrhtan awurpan,   nu se geworden is
>   hwommona heagost   (ParPs 117/21)

In two cases the relative member takes initial position, and this type is marked by some form of correlation: 'þæt . . . þæt' Chr 258, 'þa . . . hi' ParPs 125/5.[8] Thus:

>   Þæt ðu, waldend, ær
>   blode gebohtes,   þæt se bealofulla
>   hyneð heardlice,   ond him on hæft nimeð   (Chr 258)

The question of mood in these concessions is a simple matter; the verb in the dependent member is indicative or indeterminate, and there is no evidence of the subjunctive being introduced because of the concessive function.

We come now to the consideration of source material and parallel versions. In Gen 802 the relative clause, 'þæs wit begra ær wæron

---

8. Cf. 'þa þe . . . ær . . . þa nu' ASC E 979.

orsorge on ealle tid,' corresponds as follows to the OS version: 'thero uuaron uuit er beðero tuom'; it is interesting to note that the reinforcing *ær* is present in the two forms. We have already seen that in Bo 24/44 a concession formed with *þeah* corresponds to a concessive relative clause in the prose; the reverse occurs at Bo 5/11 where ' seo þe ær gladu onsiene wæs ' replaces a concession formed with *þeah* and the subjunctive in the prose: ' þeah heo ær gladu wære on to locienne.' In one case, the prose version has a concessive-equivalent temporal member, ' þa ða ic him æfre . . . ,' which the versifier replaces by a relative construction, ' þe ic him æfre . . .' (Bo 2/13). In four instances, the poetic relative clause corresponds to a relative clause in the prose also, but the poet increases the concessive feeling by reinforcement, in each case apparently to meet the exigencies of meter and alliteration: Bo 22/16 *æror lange*, prose *ær*; 22/5 *sume hwile . . . æror*, prose *ær*; 20/263 *þrage nu . . . hwyle*, prose *nu*; 22/13 *oftost nu*, prose zero. In one case, Bo 13/37, there is nothing in the prose to correspond to the concessive relative member.

Burnham (pp. 67, 70f., 73) draws attention to the parallelism between Latin and OE in the use of concessive-equivalent relative clauses. Most of the examples in ParPs correspond to the Latin forms without much change, a case in point being 125/5. In one case (68/5) the Latin only differs in having the relative clause placed initially where the OE keeps to the usual practice of final position. In three other cases (75/5, 105/18, 117/21) the only difference is that the concessive feeling is increased in the OE by the introduction (partly no doubt for metrical reasons) of *hwilon*, *ær*, *ær* respectively, which have no parallel in the Latin. Finally, in 105/27 the Latin has no relative clause and no concession; the meaning is, ' shed innocent blood,' and this is expanded in the OE to, ' shed the blood of children although they were innocent.' It may be stated that there is no evidence of the influence of Latin syntax on the OE expressions in this type of concession.

To sum up, we have found that concessive-equivalent relative members occupy a considerable position in the scheme of OE concessive constructions; about 5 per cent of all concessions are formed in this way, and there is no difference between prose and poetic usage in this respect. Relative members in this function have indicative verbs and frequently contain a reinforcing element, especially *ær*, which is sometimes correlated with a particle in the nondependent member. Neither in word order nor in mood, however, do concessive relative clauses differ from nonconcessive ones. The concessive member usually follows the nondependent member to which it is related, but sometimes is placed medially within it and in a few cases precedes it; sometimes parallel concessive members are subordinated to a single nondependent member. Source study reveals interesting interchange between concessions formed with *þeah* and relative member concessions, and we see also the heightening of concessive feeling by reinforcement over the form of the relative concessive clauses in the source, whether it be Latin or OE. Apart from the latter feature, there is close correspondence between the concessive-equivalent relative members in both languages.

12. CONCESSIVE-EQUIVALENT CLAUSES OF MANNER (*swa*-MEMBERS)

The second biggest class of concessive-equivalent constructions is that with members introduced by *swa*. A moment's pause is perhaps necessary to justify our calling *swa*-members 'concessive-equivalent,' because many grammarians treat *swa* as an autonomous concessive conjunction. Mossé, for example, ranks *swa* with *þeah* as a concessive subordinator,[9] and Burnham (p. 14) likewise puts it second only to *þeah* at the beginning of her study; she later refers to it as "a true concessive conjunction as opposed to those merely adapted to concessive use" (p. 74). It is true that the concessive functions of *swa* are considerable; we have seen it reinforcing *þeah* as well as operating in the indefinite concessive constructions, but in none of these can it be shown to have a specific concessive sense. Despite the prominent place Burnham gives it, she is by no means happy about concessive *swa* in actual use; her first and most convincing example is not from her prose material but Gen 391, and she goes on to say that "in both prose and verse the Old English construction with *swa* is somewhat ill-defined, and is rather *convertible into a concessive clause than distinctly marked as such*" (p. 14; italics mine).

If one considers each dependent *swa*-member on its own merits in relation to the context, it seems certain that *swa* is never an autonomous concessive connective but always basically introduces a clause of manner and retains this function when the member is being used concessively. Kellner is apparently of the same opinion when he says that "Adverbial Clauses relating to Manner and Degree . . . are also used in a concessive sense," quoting Gen 391.[1] A. G. Brodeur is most insistent that

---

9. *Vieil-Anglais* §186.
1. *Historical Outlines* §§127–8; Mensing reckons MHG *so* as a concessive equivalent (see *Untersuchungen* 74), and Holthausen similarly analyzes the function of OS *so* (*Altsächs. Element.* §535 anm.).

OE *swa* should not be interpreted except as 'under such circumstances';[2] Hans-Oskar Wilde, too, is dubious about Burnham's classification, and after discussing it concludes that the concessive function of *swa* is a derived one and that in general *swa* has modal value and introduces modal clauses.[3]

Although *so* occurs as a concessive conjunction in late OHG, in MHG, and in OS,[4] concessive *swa* occurs in only " a few cases " in OE prose (Burnham, p. 14). In OE poetry it occurs 32 times, the distribution being as follows: Gen 4 (1 in Gen B), Ex 1, Dan 1, ChrSat 1, And 2, Hom Frag I 1, El 2, Chr 2, Az 1, Ph 1, Vain 1, Rid 4, ParPs 6, Bo 1, Prayer 1, Beo 3. For example:

> Ic þe æne abealh, ece drihten,
> þa wit Adam twa eaples þigdon
> þurh næddran nið, swa wit na ne sceoldon.
> (ChrSat 408)

> breost innan weoll
> þeostrum geþoncum, swa him geþywe ne wæs.
> (Beo 2331)

Apart from these 32 cases which seem indisputable, there are at least two examples of *swa*, the interpretation of which is dubious:

> Scyld wel gebearg
> life ond lice læssan hwile
> mærum þeodne, þonne his myne sohte,
> ðær he þy fyrste forman dogore
> wealdan moste, swa him wyrd ne gescraf
> hreð æt hilde. (Beo 2570)

There is much controversy over the interpretation of the last three lines; Klaeber (ed., p. 216) suggests that the *swa*-member means 'but fate decreed otherwise'; this does not seem convincing, and it is energetically condemned by Meroney who interprets *swa* as belonging to a result member without concessive or adversative function (JEGPh xli.201–9).

The second doubtful passage is as follows:

> bið eal þes ginna grund gleda gefylled,
> reþra bronda, swa nu rixiað
> gromhydge guman, gylpe strynað,

---

2. 'Climax of the Finn Episode' 290; cf. also Ericson's excellent study, *Use of swa* 62f.
3. 'Aufforderung, Wunsch und Möglichkeit' 330–1.
4. Behaghel, *Deutsche Syntax* III.§1424 B; Mensing, *Untersuchungen* 74; see also Behaghel, *Die Modi im Heliand* (Paderborn 1876) 47.

>   hyra hlaforde   gehlæges tilgað,
>   oþþæt hy beswicað   synna weardas,
>   þæt hi mid þy heape   helle secað   (Jud 1 12)

Mackie (*Exeter Book* 157) interprets this as follows: "All this wide expanse will be filled with glowing embers ... though cruel-hearted men now hold dominion, acquire vainglory, strive after scorn towards their Lord, until the wardens of sin entrap them ..." A concessive interpretation of the *swa*-member seems to me forced, however, since a normal modal function seems quite natural here: '... just as now ...'

The manner relationship embraces of course the result relationship,[5] and in some of the examples of concessive *swa*, the result function can be clearly felt beside the concessive one. For example:

>   stop on stræte,   (stig wisode),
>   swa him nænig gumena   ongitan ne mihte,
>   synfulra geseon.   (And 985)

In Gen 391 we find *swa* in the dependent member correlating with *þeah* in the nondependent member: 'swa he us ne mæg ænige synne gestælan ... he hæfð us þeah þæs leohtes bescyrede.'[6] This is the only example of correlation found with *swa* concessions, though a type of reinforcement occurs a few times: in Chr 984, ParPs 72/17, 105/26, Beo 1671 we have *swa*(...)*ær*, in Chr 453 *swa ... eft*, in Ph 41 *swa iu*, and in ParPs 105/32 *swa ... furðum*.

It is noteworthy that 23 of the 32 *swa*-members are negative, eight of them with stronger than minimum negation: Dan 463, ChrSat 408, And 489, 985, El 836, Rid 6/2, ParPs 72/17, Beo 2584. The very high proportion of negatives may be due to the recurrence of a particular negative pattern which as we shall see is something of a stock phrase in OE poetry, but this does not explain the strong negatives because there are relatively few in the stock phrases in question.

The recurrent *swa*-member just referred to is an expression of surprise and disapproval, 'although it was not right,' 'although we shouldn't have'; its occurrence is as follows:

>   swa wit na ne sceoldon   ChrSat 408
>   swa hie no sceoldon   El 836
>   swa ic ne sceolde   Prayer 61
>   swa hyt no sceolde   Beo 2584
>   swa hit riht ne wæs   Gen 901

---

5. Cf. Curme, *Syntax* 286f.

6. Note that this is in Gen B, and that in OS there existed the corresponding concessive construction *so ... thoh*.

swa hit ryht ne wæs	Vain 61 [7]
swa gerysne ne wæs	Gen 1564
swa hit gedefe ne wæs	ParPs 105/22
swa hit gedefe ne wæs	Bo 26/90
swa him geþywe ne wæs	Beo 2331

The last example is not quite true to type, since it is not moral disapproval but only disapproval of irregularity, 'although this wasn't usual with him.'

Parallel *swa*-members subordinated in a single concession to one nondependent member are rare, but in Ex 80 we have two *swa*-members in such a situation, both with finite verbs but without repetition of the *swa* in the second member.

In every case *swa* heads its member, the word order thereafter being mainly *subject–object/complement–verb*, with a fair number having *object/complement–subject–verb* (thus for example And 985). There are scattered instances of other arrangements: for example, *verb–subject* Rid 2/1, *object–verb–subject* Dan 463.

It is normal for the *swa*-member to follow its related member; this obtains in a score of cases throughout the material—in Gen, Ex, Dan, ChrSat, And, HomFrag 1, El, Chr, Az, Vain, ParPs, Bo, and Beo. In a few cases, the *swa*-member is placed medially in the nondependent member: Gen 901, El 836, Rid 2/1, 6/2, ParPs 119/5, Prayer 61, Beo 2584. In at least three cases the *swa*-member takes initial position: Gen 391 (where it correlates with a *þeah*-member), Chr 984, Ph 41. There is one doubtful case:

      and him selfa sceaf
 reaf of lice. Swa gerysne ne wæs,
 læg þa limnacod.   (Gen 1564)

Thus the punctuation of ASPR 1. Very few *swa*-members however are found taking initial position, and there is no other instance of the 'disapproving' type doing so. Rather, in El 836, Beo 2584, and in Gen itself (901), among others, we find the 'disapproving' member placed medially. In the present instance, 'læg þa limnacod' is in the nature of a variation of the member preceding the *swa*-clause, and it would be more in accord with the general pattern of these concessions to put a comma instead of a stop after *lice*.[8]

The mood of the verbs in *swa*-members is indicative or indeterminate; there is no indication of the subjunctive being introduced by reason

---

7. Cf. the relative member in Maldon 190; 'þe hit riht ne wæs.'
8. So Grein-Wülker, *Bibliothek* II.390. At the same time, according to the punctuation of this edition, there may be thought to be a concessive *swa*-member in Ex 538; this would be another example of *initial* position.

of the concessive function, and this agrees with Burnham's results (pp. 25–6).[9]

In considering parallel versions and sources, we may notice that the word order *object–verb–subject* found in Dan 463, ' swa him wiht ne sceod grim gleda nið,' is also in the other version, although the content of the member is changed slightly: ' swa hyra wædum ne scod gifre gleda nið' (Az 187, the manuscript of which omits the last word). Source study suggests that the recurrent 'disapproving' *swa*-member is a feature specifically of the poetry; in Bo 26/90, ' swa hit gedefe ne wæs ' is not found in the prose original, and the same clause occurring in ParPs 105/22 has no parallel in the Latin. It may be that the other short parenthetical *swa* concessions belong also particularly to OE poetic style, since ' swa me eðe nis ' in ParPs 119/5 is not in the Latin. For the rest of the Latin correspondences, a *swa*-member twice translates an *et*-member (ParPs 72/17, 105/32), and once it corresponds to a *verumtamen*-member (ParPs 61/3; VespPs ' ah hweðre ').

To sum up, *swa* concessions occur in both poetry and prose but seem commoner in the former, where we find some special uses of the *swa* concession, notably the 'disapproving' *swa*-member. Reinforcement occurs sparingly and correlation only once, in the part of Gen translated from OS. A high proportion of *swa*-members have negated verbs, many of them strongly negated. It is usual for *swa* to introduce its member and for the verb to come at the end; the mood of the verb is indicative; *swa*-members normally follow the related nondependent members, but a number of times they are placed medially within the nondependent members and in a few cases precede them. The study of sources suggests that certain types of *swa*-members, as noted above, are characteristic of OE poetic usage.

13. CONCESSIVE-EQUIVALENT TEMPORAL MEMBERS

As Burnham has pointed out (p. 74), temporal elements show a facility for adapting themselves to the concessive function; *cum, quand (même)* are cases in point. But we have now to consider temporal members which, while retaining their temporal significance, are used concessively. Burnham (pp. 75f.) finds examples of such members introduced by *þa (þa), siððan, mid þy, þonne, mittes* (once only) and *nu*; it is

---

[9] It is difficult to understand why Cobb ('Subjunctive Mood' 49) regards the indeterminate form *sceolde* as a 'morative subjunctive' in ' swa hyt no sceolde' Beo 2585. Parallel instances of this 'disapproving' *swa*-member have the determinate indicative form *wæs*, as we have seen above.

doubtful whether the latter should be included in this class, and she admits that she does it " Although Adams . . . regards *nu* as a causal conjunction " (p. 78); in the present study, *nu*-members will be found below among the few concessive-equivalent causal members. In the OE verse I have found concessive temporal clauses introduced only by *þonne, þa,* and *oððæt.* The *þonne*-members are distributed as follows: El 1, Ph 1, Rid 1, Wife 1, Jud 1 2, Resig 1, ParPs 1, Bo 1, Sol 1; the *þa*-members: Gen 2, Dan 1, Rood 1, Chr 4, Gl 1, ParPs 1; the *oððæt*-members: Deor 1, Rid 1. Thus, apart from a number of possible but dubious examples not included, there is a total of 22 temporal dependent members used concessively, 10 introduced by *þonne,* 10 by *þa,* and 2 by *oððæt.* For example:

>   gedo usic þæs wyrðe,   þe he to wuldre forlet,
>   þa *we heanlice   hweorfan sceoldan
>   to þis enge lond,   eðle bescyrede.
>   *MS: þe   (Chr 30)

' He admitted us to glory, when (*that is,* although) we should have been rejected.'

>   Ne swylteð he symle,   þonne syllan sceal
>   innað þam oðrum   (Rid 37/5)

'(The bellows) does not die, although he has to surrender his entrails.'

Reinforcement occurs only with *þa,* which is reinforced twice, once by *efne* (Gen 2299), once by *ær* (Chr 1156); there are six instances of correlation, five with *þa*-members and one with a *þonne*-member. We find *þa* in the dependent member correlating with *þa* in the nondependent member in Gen 2299, Rood 35, Chr 1386, 1399, ParPs 77/56; *þonne* similarly correlates with *þonne* in ParPs 119/6.

Irrespective of the subordinator, the dependent member usually follows the related nondependent member. The instances of correlation just mentioned largely coincide with the cases where the dependent member is placed initially.

Parallel dependent members grammatically subordinated to a single nondependent member are found on three occasions, and this phenomenon too is related to correlation and to the initial position of dependent members. In Chr 1386 we have three dependent *þa*-members subordinated (with correlation) to a finally placed nondependent member; in the second dependent member both *þa* and the finite verb are omitted by ellipsis. In Chr 1399 two *þa*-members are subordinated (with correlation) to a following nondependent member; the second dependent member has a verb but no *þa.* In ParPs 119/6 two *þonne*-members, the second having a verb but no *þonne,* are subordinated (with correlation) to a following nondependent member.

The mood of the 25 verbs in these temporal-concessive dependent clauses is usually indicative or indeterminate, but there are three subjunctive forms, all in *þonne*-members: *mote*, 3 p.sg.pres. (Jud 1 76); *spræce*, 1 p.sg.pret. (ParPs 119/6); *gedon*, 3 p.pl.pres. (Bo 21/25). There appears to be no notional ('real–unreal') basis for the mood distinction and no relation between the mood and either correlation or the position of the member. Burnham makes only a passing reference (p. 94) to the use of the subjunctive, and her examples seem to be all either indicative or indeterminate.

The word order in the dependent members shows the normal variations and patterns found in nonconcessive temporal clauses. There is therefore nothing to add to the studies of Fourquet and Andrew.[1]

The study of sources is possible in only three cases, and they are not of great interest. We find none of the frequency noted by Burnham (p. 74) of Latin *cum*-clauses being rendered by concessive-equivalent constructions in OE. The correlative *þa . . . þa* of ParPs 77/56 corresponds simply to a pair of *et*-members in the Latin, while the correlated initial *þonne*-member of ParPs 119/6 translates a *dum*-clause which is also placed initially but without correlation. The concessive-equivalent *þonne*-member of Bo 21/25 corresponds to a similar construction in the prose original.

To sum up, we find *þonne*, *þa*, and *oððæt* introducing concessive-equivalent dependent members; there is little difference to be seen between prose and poetic usage in this. Neither reinforcement nor correlation is common, but the latter is usually found where the dependent member is placed initially and not, as normally, in final position. Parallel dependent members occur with a single nondependent member three times. The mood of the verbs in dependent members is chiefly indicative but the subjunctive is also found.

14. CONCESSIVE-EQUIVALENT LOCAL MEMBERS

Burnham (p. 78) says that concessive dependent members relating to place are rare in the prose, and this is true of the poetry also. There are eight examples in my material, distributed as follows: El 1, Chr 2, Ruin 1, ParPs 2, Beo 1, Jud 1. For example:

>   nearusorge dreah,
>   enge rune,   þær him **M** fore
>   milpaðas mæt, modig þrægde
>   wirum gewlenced.   (El 1260)

---

1. *L'Ordre des éléments* 84f., 108f., 191, and *Syntax and Style* Ch. IIf. respectively.

'He suffered anguish, though the horse ran proudly for him.' Both reinforcement and correlation are absent. Dependent members follow their related members except on one occasion:

  þær hio forhtigað, frecnes egesan
  æniges ne þurfon.   (ParPs 52/5)

The word order in these members follows the same pattern as for nonconcessive local members, and there is nothing to add to what Fourquet says (*L'Ordre des éléments* 84f., 108f., 191).

Parallel members occur on two occasions. In El 1260 (quoted above), a preceding nondependent member has two *þær*-members related to it, both with finite verbs, though in the second member *þær* is omitted. The second *þær* is also omitted in ParPs 105/8, where again there are two parallel dependent members with finite verbs.

Six of the verbs in dependent *þær*-members are indicative,[2] one subjunctive, and the rest indeterminate. The subjunctive form is *wolde*, 2 p.sg.pret:

      þa ic þec from helle ateah,
  þær þu hit wolde sylfa siþþan gehealdan. (Chr 1493)

There is no obvious notional or other reason for the distinction which thus obtains between this and the other *þær* concessions. Burnham's prose examples have indicative or indeterminate verb forms, but she makes a passing reference to a rare use of the subjunctive (p. 94).

Source study is possible in only two cases: in ParPs 52/5 the *þær*-member corresponds to an *ubi*-member, and the irregular initial position in the OE is despite the fact that in the Latin the *ubi*-member comes at the end. In ParPs 105/8 'þær ðu ... alysdest' translates 'et liberavit.'

15. CONCESSIVE-EQUIVALENT CAUSAL MEMBERS

There are four cases in the poetry in which dependent members, though primarily bearing a causal relationship, have also a concessive relationship with their respective nondependent members; two of these concessive-equivalent causal members are introduced by *þæs* (Chr 1090, ParPs 77/11), and two by *nu* (Bo 17/16, 19). For example:

  Hwy ge eow for æþelum up ahebben,
  nu on þæm mode bið monna gehwilcum
  þa rihtæþelo þe ic ðe recce ymb   (Bo 17/19)

---

2. In ASC E 1011 there is a piece of 'verse' not included in ASPR vi, which has a dependent concessive-equivalent *þær*-member also containing an indicative verb.

'Why take pride in your nobility since (*sc.* after all) everyone else is noble?' Burnham has no examples of causal members as such being used concessively, but she includes examples like the foregoing with her temporal clauses; as we have said above (IV.13), the present classification seems more satisfactory.

All four of the examples of this type of member follow the members to which they are related; within three of the members the order *subject–object/complement–verb* obtains, and the exception has been quoted above. Three of the members have indicative verbs, while that in the fourth is indeterminate. In ParPs 77/11 the *þæs*-member corresponds to a Latin nondependent member without relating element and possibly without concession. In Bo 17/16 the concession formed with *nu* is similarly expressed in the prose, but there is no prose concession corresponding to the *nu* construction in 17/19.

16. CONCESSIVE-EQUIVALENT SUBSTANTIVE MEMBERS

Burnham points out (p. 33) that the 'even' concession expressed by *si* in 'quid mirum si,' 'non mirum est si' is usually conveyed in OE by *þeah*: 'nis hit nan wundor þeah þu sy god and ic yfel.' In OE verse, *þeah* is not used in this type of environment; instead we find indirect questions, and noun clauses introduced by *þæt*, the concessive feeling being slight:

  Forþon nis ænig wundor hu him woruldmonna
  seo unclæne gecynd, cearum sorgende,
  hearde ondrede   (Chr 1015)

Compare also, 'Nalles sorgode hwæðer . . .' Bo 9/34.

  nis þæt nan wundor þæt hio sie wearm and ceald
                    (Bo 20/80)

Compare also Bo 28/64.

There are four other substantive members introduced by *þæt* which may be thought to have some concessive force without 'even' significance. They are in Gen 393, Chr 1396, Jud II 143, 242. For example:

  þonne bið eallum open ætsomne,
  gelice alyfed þæt man lange hæl.   (Jud II 143)

17. CONCESSIVE-EQUIVALENT DEGREE MEMBERS

There are two types of degree construction to be examined, first the 'correlative comparative construction' or 'correlated comparison' members, secondly, the 'correlative positive construction,' sometimes called 'definite degree' members.

'The more I drink, the more I thirst' is, says Burnham (p. 86), "a more emphatic way of saying, 'Although I drink, I thirst'." Despite the fact that Jespersen and others see more affinity with condition than with concession in this type of degree contrast,[3] there seems to me no doubt that Burnham is right. She quotes a number of concessive examples of the construction that occur in OE prose, but in the poetry examples that one can confidently regard as concessive are rare, amounting only to three: Gen 1324, Rid 47/5, Maldon 312. For example:

>   þæt is syndrig cynn;
> symle bið þy heardra   þe hit hreoh wæter,
> swearte sæstreamas   swiðor beatað.   (Gen 1324)

The three examples are analyzed below with the symbols s for subject, v for verb, o for direct or indirect object, c for complement, and comp for comparative:

(s) v *þy* comp   *þe* s o comp v   Gen 1324
s v *þy* comp   *þe* s o v   Rid 47/5
s v *þe* comp, s *þe* comp, s v *þe* comp   *þe* s v   Maldon 312

Thus the concessive member follows the nondependent member, the latter having a comparative, the former not necessarily. The verbs in the concessive members have indicative or indeterminate form.

In OE prose, the normal construction is with correlative *swa . . . swa*, not recorded in the verse in this function. Thus Burnham (p. 86) quotes from Wærferð's *Dialogues* a typical example: 'Swa ic swyþor drince, swa me swyþor þyrsteð.' In ASC there are three correlated comparison concessions, formed as follows:

swa s comp v   *swa* s comp v   E 999
swa s comp v   *swa* s v comp o   E 1086
þe comp s v o   *þe* comp s v c   E 1140

In connection with the latter, Burnham remarks, "In Old English,

---

[3] See especially *Mod.Engl.Gr.* v.21.72 and 'System of Clauses' 167; some correlated comparisons on this pattern (for example, 'the more, the merrier') can only, of course, be interpreted as conditional.

although ðy is much used with comparatives, it is only beginning to invade the correlative construction. I have found only one instance . . . of ðy in place of swa in a concessive sentence of this form" (p. 86). Far from only beginning to make its appearance in the 12th century, however, our material shows that in verse usage the þy construction is the only one found. There is thus a marked distinction between verse and prose usage in this type of concession.[4]

Before leaving the correlative comparative construction, it is interesting to note that in Bo 21/25 we have a functional combination of this construction with a concessive-equivalent temporal member, under which head this example has been included:

<pre>
                    ac hi swiðor get
monna gehwelces   modes eagan
ablendað on breostum,   þonne hi hi beorhtran gedon.
</pre>

We turn now to the correlative positive construction which is found to have weak concessive function four times in OE poetry. This type of concession has the ' even ' meaning and corresponds to NE expressions like ' I want to go far, even as far as my father has.' The OE examples occur in Gen 2554, And 332, 1232, and Bo 16/8. For example:

<pre>
                Bearwas wurdon
to axan and to yslan,   eorðan wæstma,
efne swa wide   swa ða witelac
reðe geræhton   rum land wera.   (Gen 2554)
</pre>

All four examples are formed with *efne* (or *emne*) *swa wide*, and the dependent members follow their related nondependent members, two having indicative verbs and two having verbs of indeterminate form. There is no concession in the prose corresponding to Bo 16/8, and we have no other source or parallel version to consider.

To sum up, the correlative comparative construction is used concessively a few times; in the prose until very late the construction is always *swa . . . swa*, in the poetry it is always *þy . . . þe*, but there is variety of word order in both materials. The correlative positive construction is used with weak ' even ' concessive function four times in the poetry. Neither of these concessive-equivalent degree constructions uses the subjunctive.

---

4. On the concessive use of the comparative, see also above, II.2, III.12, and below, IV.20.

18. CONCESSIVE AND CONCESSIVE-EQUIVALENT WORDS AND PHRASES

We come finally to the group of concessive expressions which, while being the most economical and in many ways the most convenient ones, are at the same time the most difficult to analyze. We must however try to maintain our distinction between those words and phrases on the one hand which, having a specific concessive function, do not at the same time serve another approximately equal function, and on the other hand those that derive their concessive function *ad hoc* from the context, preserving meanwhile other syntactical functions.

This is no easy matter. It is not easy when we try to analyze our own speech in such terms; to quote two examples suggested by Curme (*Syntax* 339–40), we have to do with the difference between the concessions in:

> His wife clung to him with all his faults.
> This old woman dolls herself up like a young flapper.

In the first sentence the expression 'with all his faults' has only a concessive function, and *with* does not have its normal function of indicating accompaniment. We can demonstrate this by substituting *wealth* for *faults*; when we do this, the sentence no longer makes satisfactory sense because we expect the words 'with all his . . .' to introduce some surprising factor despite which the statement is true. In the second example, on the other hand, the concession depends entirely on the added significance we give to the words 'old woman' over and above their primary function as subject of the sentence. By special intonation we can make 'this old woman' mean 'this woman, although she is old,' but we can also say the sentence without this concessive overtone, and if we replace *old woman* by *girl* the sentence does not become at all structurally odd. In other words, there is nothing about the wording of this second sentence that is inherently concessive; the words *old woman* form a concessive-equivalent group.

The concessive function of individual words and phrases has been discussed incidentally by various scholars; in the case of NE one might perhaps mention Schubiger's researches on intonation in connection with relational expression ('I'd do *that* to get the children bread').[5] For ME the phenomenon has been noticed by Einenkel,[6] and for OE we have such studies as those of Chase and Callaway on

---

5. *Role of Intonation* 29f.
6. Cf. especially *Geschichte* II.21f.

participipial functions.[7] Above all we have Chapter VIII of Burnham's book, which summarizes the main features of concessions formed by single words and phrases in OE prose. According to her, "notwithstanding the large adoption of the absolute and of the appositive participle" (*sc.* "from Latin"), "condensed concessions are somewhat rare." The poetic material shows very different results: about one-fifth of all the concessions found are formed with single words and phrases, and relatively few of them are participial constructions.

The greater part of the material consists of concessive-equivalent examples and these will be presented first. The few words and phrases which seem to have an autonomous concessive function will be treated individually later.

We can conveniently divide up the concessive-equivalent material according to whether the examples have 'even' significance or not.

19. CONCESSIVE-EQUIVALENT ELEMENTS WITHOUT 'EVEN' SIGNIFICANCE

There are 127 examples to be classed under this head and they are distributed as follows: Gen 14 (2 in Gen B), Ex 2, Dan 1, And 11, Soul I 1, El 9, Chr 16, Gl 6, Ph 2, Jul 9, Wid 2, Order 1, Prec 1, Whale 2, Soul II 1, Rid 14, Wife 1, Hell 1, Ruin 2, ParPs 5, Bo 5, Max II 1, Jud II 1, Charm 2/1, Beo 17, Jud 1. These figures aim at completeness without the sacrifice of objectivity; a number of examples could not be included because their concessive nature was in doubt.

The great variety of elements that occur in concessive function makes a wholly systematic classification very difficult, but a few features stand out as significant.

Undoubtedly the majority of the elements are appositive words and phrases; for example:

Ða ic, womma leas, yfel earfeþu	wite þolade,	(Chr 1451)
þæt ic . . . ofer *meodubence wordum wrixlan.	Lyt ic wende æfre sceolde muðleas sprecan, *MS: meodu	(Rid 60/7)
feorhbennum seoc	Ic ðæs ealles mæg gefean habban	(Beo 2739)

Compare in OE prose: 'Her wæs Ecgbriht abbud unscyldig ofslegen'

7. See Bibliography 2, s.nn.

ASC C 916. It seems characteristic of these concessive appositions to follow immediately the word to which they relate, and there may well have been special intonation on the appositive elements to point the concession. We have 'þu ellþeodig' Gen 2680, 'ðu feasceaft' Gen 2822, 'wer wintrum geong' Gen 2889, 'þu hygecræftig' Order 25, and many others illustrating this order, but occasionally too we find the concessive elements placed in front; 'eadiges orhlytte' And 680, 'unsynnum' Beo 1072, 'forstrangne' Rid 50/4 are cases in point. We also find the pattern *swa plus appositive adjective or participle*; this occurs 10 times, for example:

<pre>
                    Sie ðe, mægena god,
þrymsittendum   þanc butan ende,
þæs ðu me swa meðum   ond swa manweorcum
þurh þin wuldor inwrige   wyrda geryno.   (El 809)
</pre>

There are many concessive-equivalent prepositional phrases. Several of these have their concessive value determined entirely by the context, for example:

<pre>
                    Is us þearf micel
þæt we mid heortan   hælo secen,
þær we mid gæste   georne gelyfað
þæt þæt hælobearn   heonan up stige
mid usse lichoman,   lifgende god.   (Chr 751)
</pre>

'. . . although with human frame . . .' But in many, the meaning of the preposition contributes to the concessive function; this is especially so with *butan* and *ofer*.

The preposition *butan* occurs in a number of concessive phrases both in poetry and prose.[8] In all the poetic examples, *butan* quite clearly preserves its meaning 'without': 'Ic gefrægn . . . hring endean . . . butan tungan' Rid 48/1. At times in OE prose, however, *butan* comes near to being an autonomous concessive element: 'bead þa Swegen full gild . . . 7 buton þam hi hergodan swa oft swa hi woldon' ASC E 1013.

The meanings 'against, in contravention of, contrary to, beyond,' which are well established for *ofer* throughout OE,[9] enable *ofer* to pass easily into the function of a concessive preposition, 'despite.' In Burnham's study (p. 110), as here, *ofer* is classed as a concessive-equivalent preposition, but some of the examples may suggest that at times it could be used as an autonomous concessive element in contexts where its other senses are precluded. The examples, after drastically eradi-

---

8. See Burnham, p. 116. On *butan* as a relating element, see above, III.6.
9. Cf. BT, BTS, Clark Hall's *Dictionary*, s.v.

cating the more dubious cases, total 24 and are distributed as follows: Gen 3 (1 in Gen B), Ex 1, Dan 1, And 4, El 2, Chr 1, Gl 1, Ph 2, Jul 4, Prec 1, Whale 1, Beo 3. For example:

>   He ofer willan giong
> to ðæs ðe he eorðsele   ænne wisse   (Beo 2409)
> ne habbað wiht for þæt,   þeah hi wom don
> ofer meotudes bibod.   (Prec 70)

Compare in the prose: '7 him þær togeanes com Pallig . . . forþam þe he asceacen wæs fram Æðelrede cyncge ofer ealle ða getrywða ðe he him geseald hæfde, 7 eac se cyng him wel ʒegifod hæfde on hamon, 7 on golde' ASC A 1001.

Perhaps the best example is in Ex 61, but this depends on the interpretation of a *hapax legomenon*: 'Moyses ofer þa, fela meoringa, fyrde gelædde.' It is usual to interpret *meoringa* as 'hindrances,' related to OE *gemearr* 'obstacle,' Gothic *gamarzeins*, and if this is so, *ofer* must mean 'despite' rather than physically 'over, beyond.' Klaeber's note on the following occurrence of *ofer* is worth mentioning: 'Biowulf maþelode—he ofer benne spræc, wunde wælbleate' Beo 2724. While denying that *ofer* means 'in spite of,' Klaeber points out that "The original, local sense of *ofer*: 'over the wound' easily passes into the modal one: 'wounded as he was'." [1]

In its temporal function, the preposition *be* occurs in Gl 1234: 'bi me lifgendum'; 'be him lifgendum' is likewise used concessively in ASC A718. In ParPs 77/31 we have the phrase 'in eallum . . . þissum' which, although a straightforward translation of 'in omnibus his' (VespPs 'in allum ðissum'), seems to combine with the temporal function a concessive one like that of 'for eallum þissum' in ASC.

Past and present participial phrases occur 12 times,[2] mainly combining temporal and concessive function. For example:

> of lice ateah   liodende ban,
> wer unwundod   (Gen 182)
> ac Offa geslog   ærest monna,
> cnihtwesende,   cynerica mæst.   (Wid 38)

---

1. Ed., p. 220; see also *Archiv* civ. 287f. and cf. Cosijn, *Anteekeningen op den Beowulf* (Leiden 1892) 37.

2. My examples do not all coincide with those of Callaway (see Bibliography 2, s.n.), and Burnham (p. 118) is similarly unable to agree with all his interpretations. Nor from my material (cf. Wid 38, quoted here) can I agree that the concessive use of the appositive participle is directly from the Latin (see 'The Appositive Participle' 282–3, 304–5). The sole verse example with which he seeks to prove this (*winnende* Bo 11/34: *pugnantia*) is unfortunate since it makes him assume a relationship between the alliterative *Meters* and their ultimate Latin source which is not thought to exist.

DEPENDENT CONCESSIONS WITHOUT þeah IV.20

>   . . . hiora æghwilc   wið oðer winð,
>   and þeah winnende   wreðiað fæste   (Bo 11/33)

'. . . and yet, though at strife, support each other'; the prose has simply '7 þeah wræðeð oðer.'

There are no examples in OE poetry of a participle used concessively in a 'dative absolute' construction, but there is one instance of a dative absolute concessive phrase without participle; it occurs in both versions of Soul (I 62, II 57) in almost the same form:

>   ond þe þin sawl sceal
>   minum *unwillum   oft gesecan
>   *MS: unwillu   (Soul I 62)

'. . . and I, thy soul, have oft to seek thee, though against my will.'

There is little of interest to be learnt from the study of the sources of ParPs and Bo. It will be remembered that in dealing with the þeah concessions, we found that a dependent member introduced by þeah þe in ParPs 68/31 had translated a concessive-equivalent phrase in the Latin. Latin indeed developed a facility for expressing concession by this means more than OE ever achieved, and it is no surprise to find that the four concessive-equivalent phrases in ParPs are direct translations from the Latin which likewise uses only the context to show that they are concessive. Two of the Bo examples are also similarly expressed in its source, the other three being absent from the prose.

To sum up, concessive-equivalent words and phrases without 'even' significance occur frequently and in a variety of forms in OE poetry. They are chiefly appositive, in the majority of cases following immediately the word they qualify. When they are adjectives or participles, they are sometimes preceded by *swa*. There are numerous prepositional phrases, especially with *butan* and *ofer*, and several participial concessions (some in texts not based on Latin originals), but none in dative absolute constructions; the only dative absolute used concessively is *minum unwillum*.

20. CONCESSIVE-EQUIVALENT ELEMENTS WITH 'EVEN' SIGNIFICANCE

There are many words and phrases which, conditioned by the context, build up a concessive climax or, as we have called it, an 'even' concession. Since it is impossible to see in these words any inherent concessive meaning, we class them together as concessive-equivalents, but functionally they should not be divorced from other ' even ' concessions, whether formed with *gyt* or *þeah*, as we have seen above, or with *wiht*, as we shall see below. With ' even ' concessions it is easier to be subjective than with other types of concession; in collecting the following examples special care has been taken to exclude all but those which it is hoped would be recognized as concessive by any functional investigator. Even so, there are as many as 52 examples, distributed as follows: Gen 9 (2 in Gen B), Ex 1, Dan 1, ChrSat 1, And 1, El 2, Chr 5, Gl 2, Jul 8, Wand 1, Gift 1, Panther 1, Soul II 2, Deor 1, Rid 1, ParPs 1, Bo 12, Sol 1, Prayer 1.

As with the material in the previous section, there is here an embarrassing variety of forms taken by the concessive elements. There are however a number of outstanding recurrent features. Certain words like *an, agen, sylf* [3] readily take on a concessive coloring, as we see in the following examples:

>   Wa la, ahte minra handa geweald
> and moste ane tid   ute weorðan,
> wesan ane winterstunde,   þonne ic . . .   (Gen 368)[4]

> Eala, ofermodan,   hwi eow a lyste
> mid eowrum swiran   selfra willum
> þæt swære gioc   symle underlutan?   (Bo 10/18)

Sometimes the concessive climax is pointed by *furður, furðum*:

> Ic þec halsige,   hlæfdige min,
> Iuliana . . .
> þæt þu furþur me   fracepu ne wyrce,
> edwit for eorlum,   þonne þu ær dydest   (Jul 539)

Compare in the prose: ' þ ne stod furðon ænne monað ' ASC E 1010. On several occasions a series of *ne . . . ne . . . (ne)* or *ge . . . ge* is used for this purpose:

> Næs hyra wlite gewemmed,   ne nænig wroht on hrægle,
> ne feax fyre beswæled   (Dan 436)

Compare in the prose: ' he lið inne unforbærned mid his magum 7 freondum monað, ge hwilum twegen ' Oros 20/20. So too, *eac*; in the contrast between the way in which men ignore God while beasts and nature acknowledge Him, we read:

>   Hwæt, eac sæ cyðde
> hwa hine gesette   on sidne grund,
> tirmeahtig cyning   (Chr 1163)

---

3. Cf. ' I thought Heathcliff himself less guilty than I' *Wuthering Heights* 230.
4. Note that *winter-* carries concessive feeling as well as *ane*.

Sometimes these climax-forming elements combine; thus, *ge eac* Chr 1169. We also find *efne* used in these concessions, and in Bo this occurs six times; for example:

> Hafað fæder engla   fyr gebunden
> efne to þon fæste   þæt hit fiolan ne mæg
> eft æt his eðle   (Bo 20/153)

The climax effect is occasionally produced with comparatives, and once ('Þonne beoð þy hefigran' Wand 49) with the instrumental *þy* as well; this reminds us of the concessive-equivalent degree members already dealt with. For example:

> Ic eom on stence   strengre *micle
> þonne ricels   oþþe rose . . .   *MS deest
>   (Rid 40/23)

In a few cases *eall* is the significant element:

> Swylce ic næfre on eallum þam fyrngewrytum   findan ne mihte
> soðe *samnode.   *MS: samode   (Sol 8)

'. . . even in the whole of . . .' Similarly, Soul II 71. See also below, IV.23. In Bo 9/23 *on uppan* is used, and in Gen 1580 *huru*:

>   are ne wolde
> gesceawian,   ne þa sceonde huru
> hleomagum helan

In several examples, however, we cannot point to the special influence of any particular word and the concession is made by the context alone.

We come now to the sources and parallel versions. In ParPs 77/19, 'þa . . . furþur' translates 'et . . . adhuc' (VespPs '7 . . . ðaget'). Although Bo uses *efne* six times in 'even' concessions, this use of *efne* does not derive from the prose original in a single instance: in 20/153, 26/62, 28/28 there is no corresponding concession in the prose; the prose corresponding to 22/16 and 24/57 forms the 'even' concession without *efne*; in 20/122, where the verse has *efne*, the prose has *eft* in concessive function. In two further cases, 10/18 'selfra willum,' 30/11 'furðum,' the corresponding prose has no concession. In 8/31, 33, concessions expressed with 'furðum' are so expressed also in the prose; in 9/23, 30 'on uppan agene broðor and his modor,' 'his bryde ofslog self' appear in the prose as 'ge furðon his agene modor, 7 his agene broðor,' 'ge furðon his agen wif' respectively. Some of these changes were obviously carried out to solve metrical difficulties and have no syntactical significance beyond demonstrating the range of expressions considered approximately equivalent; the introduction of ' even ' concession for no obvious reason except to make a line metrically acceptable can be paralleled in the later ballads. On the other hand, the marked difference with regard to *efne* is noteworthy.

To sum up, in the formation of these ' even ' concessions, certain elements recur, such as *an, agen, sylf, furður, eac, efne*, and the climaxes are also formed with *ne . . . ne, ge . . . ge* and the comparative forms of adjectives. Most of these types occur in prose and verse alike, but in studying the source of Bo we observe that the prose does not use *efne* in the six cases where it is found in the poetic version.

21. THE CONCESSIVE USE OF *wiht*

The OE word *wiht* was used in various indefinite locutions which, besides leading to the formation of the indefinite pronouns *aught* and *nought*, were ways of emphasizing a point with such force as to exclude all possibility of denial. In these expressions *wiht* seems to have a marked concessive flavor corresponding to the colloquial asseverations *whatever, at all, in the slightest,* and the like today.[5] Although in its weakest form, ' It's no trouble whatever ' means no more than the simple negative, ' It's no trouble,' according to the degree of our fervor we impart to it the underlying meaning ' even in the slightest.'

This kind of concessive feeling is present in examples like the following:

<blockquote>
Ne meahte ic æt hilde   mid Hruntinge
wiht gewyrcean   (Beo 1659)
Ne bið him on þam wicum   wiht to sorge   (Ph 611)
Oft hie to bote   balde gecwædon
þæt hie þæs wiges   wihte ne rohton   (Dan 200)
</blockquote>

' They often went so far as to say they didn't care a straw for the image.'

Thus it is clear that functionally *wiht* cannot be separated from other words (like *furðum*) which lend themselves to ' even ' concession. On the other hand, *wiht* forms a class apart in its wide distribution, its morphological and syntactical adaptability, and above all in the acute problem of interpretation that it presents. Since this latter problem is intimately connected with the various forms and syntactical functions of *wiht*, we shall postpone the question of the limits of its concessive use until after we have fully described the details of distribution.

5. Cf. BT, Grein's *Sprachschatz*, s.v. *wiht* III and 2 respectively.

In its various forms and combinations, WHIT [6] occurs 179 times in OE verse. There are three main distinctions of form, corresponding to NE *whit, aught, nought,* and cutting across these we may distinguish several categories according to the syntactical function of the form.

As subject of a verb or complement of a link-verb, *wiht* (as in Chr 1053) or its by-form *wuht* (as in Gen 812) occurs 19 times. In the same functions, the compound *awiht* as in Gen 1904 (or its by-forms *owiht* as in Dan 273, *oht* Chr 238, *aht* Jud II 205, *auht* Bo 6/6) occurs 16 times. On the other hand, *nawiht* (Jud II 201, *naht* Sol 258) occurs in these capacities only twice.

The accusative use of these three forms is much commoner, that is, in objective function (as in Gen 242) and adverbially as 'accusative of measure' (as in Jud II 33). With its by-form *wuht* (as in Gen 529), *wiht* occurs 35 times; *awiht* (as in ParPs 76/2) occurs 37 times, the by-forms being *awuht,* as in Gen 496, *owiht* Chr 921, *awyht* ParPs 91/14, *aht* ParPs 143/4, *auht* Bo 11/7; and with by-forms *nowiht,* as in Rid 11/5, *nauht* Bo 13/25, *naht* Jud II 207, *nawiht* occurs 6 times. There is also the form *nanuht* in Fasting 156, which brings the total to 7 in accusative functions.[7]

The dative form *wihte,* as in Rid 47/5, or *wuhte,* as in Gen 681, occurs 33 times, *owihte* (And 800), *auhte* (Bo 16/20) only 7 times, and there are no dative forms at all of *nawiht,* outside prepositional phrases.

The use of the genitive is confined to three instances: *owihtes* Dan 428, *nahtes* Fasting 109, 126.

The prepositional phrases are as follows. There are three examples of *for wiht(e)* (Gen, ParPs, Beo), and four of *for awiht* (ParPs only). For example:

>   no he him *þa sæcce ondred,
> ne him þæs wyrmes wig   for wiht dyde
>   *MS: þā   (Beo 2347)

There is one example of *to wuhte* (Gen 838) and six of *to na(wi)hte* (ParPs, Bo), one instance of *be wihte* ('Nat ic hit be wihte' Pharoah 4) and one of *be owihte* (ParPs 72/17); *mid wihte* occurs three times, all in Gen B, for example:

---

6. We are not of course interested in NED WIGHT, the more material sense of *wiht* ('Ic eom wunderlicu wiht' Rid 18/1). The semantic distinction is usually easy to make, and examples like the following when it is blurred are rare: 'Nele hio forlætan libbendes wuht' Bo 13/33.

7. One does not of course include *naht-* in the compound *nahtfremmendra* (ParPs 58/2, FragPs 69).

                    swa ic mid wihte ne mæg
of þissum lioðobendum.   (Gen 381)

Finally, in Seaf 46 there is *ymbe owiht*.[8]

There are no data published, similar to the above, concerning the occurrence of WHIT in OE prose. Having established, therefore, in a brief survey that ASC was fairly representative of general prose usage in this respect, I examined the forms and functions of WHIT throughout the annals and the results are presented below in table form so that they may be compared with those for the poetry. Three marked differences appear. ASC is without a single example of the simple form *wiht*, whereas in the verse there are more examples of this than of the *awiht* and *nawiht* forms put together. Secondly, there are no uncontracted forms of the compounds *awiht* and *nawiht*; ASC has *aht-*, *naht-*, *noht-*, whereas in the verse the compound forms rarely obscure the *-wiht-* element; significantly enough, the only poetic text which largely contracts the compound forms is Bo. Thirdly, while in the verse there are 163 forms not compounded with the negative particle against 19 compound negative forms, in ASC there are only 6 positive (*aht*) against 35 negative forms.[9]

Statistical Summary: Poetry

	wiht	*awiht*	*nawiht*	Totals
Nom.	19	16	2	37
Accus.	35	37	7	79
Gen.	—	1	2*	3
Dat.	33	7	—	40
Prepos.phrase	8	6	6	20
Totals	95	67	19	179

8. We may note also the *hapax legomenon* in Gen 1953, *æt edwihtan*; whatever the etymology, the phrase has the same 'even' concessive function as the *wiht*-phrases:

                        næfre *hleowlora
    æt edwihtan   æfre weorðeð
    feorhberendra forht and acol
                        *MS: hleor lora   (Gen 1953)

9. In view of these differences, it is interesting to find in one of the ASC Poems (annal 1065, MSS C, D) a simple *wiht*-form:

                        wihte ne agælde
        þæs þe þearf wæs   þæs þeodkyninges.   (DeathEdward 33)

ASC

	wiht	awiht	nawiht	Totals
Nom.	—	1	6	7
Accus.	—	1	24	25
Gen.	—	2	1	3
Dat.	—	—	—	—
Prepos.phrase	—	2	1	3
Totals	—	6	32	38

The problem now arises of distinguishing between concessive and nonconcessive uses of *wiht*. There are many cases where the indefinite concessive feeling is quite clear:

> Nis me wiht æt eow
> leofes gelong, ne ge me laþes wiht
> gedon motun. (Gl 312)

We have already looked at several other equally clear examples. At the same time there are many instances where the concessive feeling is small, and this is particularly noticeable with the compound negative forms. The stages are infinite between ' Ic þæs nowiht wat ' Rid 11/5, ' I don't in the slightest know,' where there is some concessive feeling, and ' nose habbað, nawiht gestincað ' ParPs 134/17, where *nawiht* is perhaps little more than an emphatic ' nothing,' but concessive feeling seems less readily expressed through the compound negative form. The four examples of *to na(wi)hte* in ParPs correspond to a scarcely concessive *ad nihilum*, with little to show that the translator intended special asseverative force. In the prose of ASC, where there seems to be a marked absence of concessive feeling in the forms of WHIT, it is significant that 86 per cent of them are contracted forms of *nawiht*. Most of these are to be translated simply by one of the NE cognate forms, *nought* or *not*: ' Titus. . . sæde þæt he þone dæg forlure þe he noht to gode on ne gedyde ' A 81; ' þa nolde se papa naht þ don ' F 995; 'hit naht ne beheold ' E 1006; 'he ne gefremede naht biscoplices ' D 1050. Burnham indeed makes no mention of the concessive function of *wiht*, so it seems quite certain that in the prose as a whole this function is, to say the least, less marked and less common than in the verse. At the same time, it appears from BT that concessive use of *wiht* is not altogether unknown in OE prose; even in ASC, there are three instances (for example, F 992) where a concessive function seems quite likely in contracted forms of *awiht*.

It is fairly certain, then, that there is a relationship between the absence of concessive feeling and the occurrence of negative contracted forms of *wiht*. It is true that *wiht* is almost always in negative contexts, but where the concessive feeling is strongest there is disjunction of the negative particle and the *wiht*-form. Moreover, even where a strong form of the negative particle (*no, na*) is compounded with the *wiht*-form, the most clearly concessive examples are without contraction, and this is true also of the *awiht* compound. This may well be because the concessive function of *wiht* was associated with stress or high musical pitch while the compound forms had secondary stress on the *-wiht* element which naturally tended to preserve its syllabic identity. Compare the stress and intonation in NE when we make *whatever* asseveratively concessive in ' It's no trouble *whatever.*' If this is true, we might distinguish concessive from nonconcessive *wiht* according to whether the forms are ' strong ' (uncontracted) or ' weak ' (contracted). It is significant perhaps that in the verse *wiht, awiht, nawiht* invariably bear metrical stress and frequently the alliteration.

We must emphasize secondly the difference between poetic and prose usage in the matter of concessive *wiht*. Instances that we can be sure are concessive are very rare in ASC while in OE verse the majority are clearly concessive and it would not be easy to say definitely that concessive feeling was entirely absent in a single case. It can hardly be a coincidence that it is in the verse that we find not only more *wiht*-forms proportionately but find them usually unnegated agglutinatively, uncompounded, and uncontracted. And we find this distinction acknowledged in the instance of *wiht* in the poem DeathEdward, embedded in the prose of ASC.

The study of sources and parallel versions is of some interest. To judge from the OS fragment of *Genesis*, the OE version is retaining a continental concessive use of *wiht*; corresponding to Gen 812, the OS reads : ' Nis unk hier uuiht biuoran . . . unk nis hier scattas uuiht.' But the position is very different when we compare the OE prose Bo with the alliterative rendering. Just as in the ASC the only full *wiht*-form occurs in a poem, so the poetic Bo incorporates many instances of *wiht* absent from the prose version; indeed the majority of the occurrences of *wiht* in the verse have no place in the prose. Especially is this so with the more obviously concessive examples; for example : ' Ne þincð me þæt wundur wuhte þe læsse ' Bo 20/117. It is significant too that where there are corresponding examples of *wiht*, the prose uses a compound negative form where the verse has more usually a positive form with a disjunctive *ne* :

Bo	6/16	auht . . . ne	Prose:	nanwuht
"	9/20	ne . . . elles wuhte	"	nanwuht
"	14/9	ne . . . wuhte	"	nanwuht

" 20/107   ne meahte ... awuht   "   nanwuht libbendes
                 libban
" 20/166   auht ne   "   nanwuht
" 21/23   auht ne   "   nauht

It can be demonstrated that the above alterations conveniently supply alliteration or at any rate fill some metrical need. But one cannot go on from this to dismiss any notion that free (*a*)*wiht*-forms as such are preferred in the poetry; if metrical adjustment were the only factor involved, one would expect to find *auht ... ne* in the prose appearing occasionally as *nauht* or the like in the poetic version, but there are no examples of this converse change.

It is possible to have a *wiht* construction in one version corresponding to an equivalent asseverative construction not employing *wiht* in another: compare Bo 22/46 'gif he awuht nafað' with the prose '... nan grot ...' This happens twice in ASC, where, however, it is more usual to have the *wiht* constructions corresponding closely in the several versions: for E 1016 *naht*, D has *nan þinc*, and for F 1036 *naht*, E has *nan þing*.

The poetic text most faithful to a Latin original at some length is ParPs, yet while this text abounds with *wiht* expressions, relatively few correspond to a similar concessive asseverative in the Latin. In 76/2, 'næs ic on þam siðe beswicen awiht' translates 'et non sum deceptus.' In a score of cases, *ne* and (*a*)*wiht* correspond to a simple negative in the Latin, but this cannot be taken as evidence that *ne ... wiht* means no more than a simple negative. Everything points to the poet's desire to strengthen his version [1] with asseverations of the 'in the slightest' kind, in the same way as the poetic Bo differs from the prose. Moreover, when the Latin itself uses stronger expressions (with or without concessive feeling), the translator finds *wiht*-forms adequate to render them; thus in 75/4 'ne þær wiht fundan' translates 'et nihil invenerunt,' in 89/5 'for wiht' translates 'pro nihilo'; compare also 105/20. In 59/11, 72/16, 17, 107/12 'to na(wi)hte' translates 'ad nihilum.' It is to be noted too that the Latin 'non timebo quid faciat mihi homo' is rendered by 'ne me wiht an siteð egesan awiht æniges mannes' (55/9) and by 'nis me ege mannes for ahwæðer' (55/4), the latter phrase making it quite clear that the poet wishes *wiht* in 55/9 to give the statement a concessive flavor.

To sum up, *wiht*, which occurs very frequently in OE verse, almost always in this material conveys a slight 'even' concession. Such concessive expression seems to be rare in prose usage and this is matched by the rarity of positive, uncontracted forms of *wiht*.

---

[1]. Cf. the similar conclusion when other constructions were compared with those in the sources, II.15, IV.20, and elsewhere.

22. *for*

In her excellent section on *for*, Burnham says, " In Old English we find a number of instances in which the meaning wavers between the causal and the concessive, but not many instances of clearly defined concessive uses " (p. 112). The same holds true for the poetic material. We have already seen, among the nondependent member concessions, that *forðon* is probably used concessively a few times, and we have also seen that *for* occurs seven times in phrases with *wiht*, serving to heighten the ' even ' concession:

>   no he . . . ondred,
> ne him þæs wyrmes wig   for wiht dyde   (Beo 2347)

Apart from these uses, *for* appears in concessive phrases five times in OE poetry: Gen 1 (not in Gen B), And 1, ParPs 3. For example:

> Onfoð þæm fæmnum,   lætað frið agon
> gistas mine,   þa ic for gode wille
> gemundbyrdan,   gif ic mot, for eow.   (Gen 2473)

It is worth pointing out that in ASC C 1013 a concession on the pattern ' for all this ' corresponds to ' buton þam ' in E.

The three ParPs examples are all of ' for (n)ahwæðer ' which is synonymous with ' for (a)wiht '; in ParPs 55/6 ' for nahwæðer nowiht ' corresponds simply to ' pro nihilo '; the other two examples consist of the same line, ' nis me ege mannes for ahwæðer,' which appears in 55/4 and 117/6, both times translating ' non timebo quid faciat mihi homo.'

23. ' all '

In OE, ' all ' has not the status of a separate concessive particle. Nevertheless, in view of its importance in concessions of later English (ME *al*, conj., NE *although, for all, all the same*),[2] it may be found useful to group in a special section the references to ' all ' when it is associated in an apparently significant way with OE concessions. Most of the references are to examples already dealt with and discussed in earlier parts of the study.

---

[2]. On the importance of *al, aleine* in dependent concessive members in MHG, see Mensing, *Untersuchungen* 60f.; on *als(o)*, cf. ibid. 74.

Burnham (p. 20f.) lists several examples of *þeah* being followed, though not immediately, by *eall*, the function of which was no doubt to reinforce the concession. She proceeds to discuss the relation of this use of *eall* to the rise of 'although' in ME. This problem is also discussed by Einenkel,[3] and more recently by Horn. The latter concludes that this OE phenomenon is indeed the precursor of 'although' and that the scholars who assume a coalescence of the two concessive conjunctions *al* and *though* are wrong. The following 'all,' as it appears in OE, became so important as a reinforcing element, he says, that it was moved to initial position.[4] One might suggest 'almost' as a parallel; this occurs as *mæst eall* and *eall mæst* within two lines in ASC C 1065.

The clearest example of 'all' reinforcing *þeah* in OE poetry is the oft-quoted 'þeah ic eal mæge' in Beo 680, but we should also compare Jul 446 and Exhort 22. In the latter we have the sequence 'þeah ... eall ... mid þæm eallum' in which, whatever the function of *eall*, there is no doubt that the prepositional phrase acts as a reinforcing element. Note also the force of 'þæs ealles' in the nondependent *þa*-concession, Chr 1496 (see above, III.9). It may be that *eall* plays a part in some of the concessive-equivalent relative member constructions, for instance ParPs 105/27.

On the concessive expression 'for all this,' Burnham observes that *all* in this group bridges the narrow gap between cause and concession; "when *for* is accompanied by *eall*, the contrast between the 'cause' referred to and its 'ineffectiveness' becomes explicit, and the meaning of the preposition shifts to 'in spite of'" (p. 114). Nevertheless, *for* can be replaced by *in* and the group can still be used concessively; thus we have, 'in eallum ... þissum' ParPs 77/31.

An adverbial use of 'all' comes near to being concessive several times. For instance:

                and afuhtan me
ealle earwunga   ungemete swyðe.   (ParPs 108/2)

The phrase 'quite without cause' is concessive-equivalent, and the 'all' gives the OE a stronger concessive meaning than the Latin has, 'et expugnaverunt me gratis.' Compare too—if the emendation is correct—'(ea)l unhlitme' in Beo 1129, which is concessive-equivalent even without *eal*, but is certainly more explicit with it. Finally, we have noticed the part played by 'all' in the concessive-equivalent words and phrases of 'even' significance; compare Soul II 71, Sol 8.

---

3. *Geschichte* II.43–4.
4. 'Untersuchungen' 219–20.

V

Conclusion

THE main features of the individual constructions have already been summarized, and it is not the intention here to repeat these summaries. The aim is rather to draw together certain factors inevitably obscured by the formal divisions of the foregoing presentation, to make observations cutting across the formal categories, and to underline characteristics the significance of which extends beyond the class in which they fall.

Five types of concession have given special difficulty in principle. There was the difficulty of analyzing the function of *ac* (III.2) and in distinguishing the concessive from the adversative and substitutive functions. The difficulty of distinguishing concession from the adversative relation was also encountered in dealing with the zero relating element construction (III.12). The line separating alternative concessions from the coordinate grouping of opposites ('He comes to see her, early and late') was likewise not easy to draw (IV.2). Nor was it easy to distinguish between indefinite concession and the nonconcessive indefinite relative construction (IV.5). Finally, there was the difficulty of determining the limits of the concessive function of *wiht* (IV.21). In the five sections referred to, we have attempted to resolve these difficulties and have discussed the theoretical basis on which the distinctions adopted have rested.

We have seen the 'challenge' construction operating the concessive relation in indefinite relative members (IV.7, 8) and in indefinite local members (IV.9). We have seen something like the 'challenge' in the use of the imperative in a few concessions formed without relating element (III.12).

The inversion of subject and verb to form a dependent concessive member (IV.3) cannot be separated from the use of such inversion in the formation of alternative concessions of the type *beo he . . . beo he*, found in OE prose.

Although *þeah* (II) and *hwæðere* (III.1) are the only particles in OE which are almost entirely confined to concessive function, the nonconcessive uses of both being rare, the importance of other single elements such as *ac* and *and* must not be underestimated. The widespread concessive use of *swa* is particularly important. While it is claimed (IV.12) that *swa* is not autonomously concessive but rather a concessive-equivalent particle, it has to be remembered that it plays an important role in reinforcing *þeah* (II.2), as well as in alternative and indefinite concessions (IV.2, 5ff.) and concessive-equivalent phrases (IV.19). Moreover, in the concessive-equivalent clauses of manner, it is used in a special recurrent pattern ('swa hit no sceolde') which we have called the 'disapproving' concession (IV.12).

Among the other stock patterns must be mentioned the 'threatened' concession with *gyt*, 'still at peace, (though later . . .),' as in Beo 1163 (III.7). Similarly there is the recurrence of 'ær oððe sið,' 'god oððe yfel,' and other alternative concessions (IV.2). In concessions formed without relating element there is the frequent pattern of a verb implying volition followed by a renunciation of its action; it is particularly common for the renouncing member to be short, with disjunctive word order: 'Him seo wen geleah' (III.12). Double concessions (where for instance the protasis of one concession is also the apodosis of another) occur with several types of concession, but it seems especially common to have one of the concessions formed without relating element (III.12).

The significance of a negated member containing *þy* and a comparative is seen in connection with *þeah* concessions (II.2), zero relating element concessions (III.12), and concessive-equivalent degree members (IV.17). Concessions as a whole commonly have a positive statement related to a negative concessive member, but this is markedly so with *þeah* (II.8), zero relating element (III.12), indefinite concessions of degree (IV.6), and concessive-equivalent clauses of manner (IV.12). It is noticeable that the negation is usually expressed strongly, with *no, na, næfre*, and the like.

In IV.18ff. we have grouped a large number of concessions formed with single words and phrases. At the same time it must be remembered that throughout the material are found concessive members, dependent and nondependent, which have no finite verb. This is particularly so with the chief poetic form of the alternative concession (IV.2) and there are a few scattered cases where a finite verb is absent, usually by ellipsis, among the concessions with *þeah* (see II.10), *hwæðere* (III.1), *ac* (III.2), *and* (III.3), *gyt* (III.7), and zero relating element (III.12).

Also occurring with several constructions is the elliptical concession, where the relation between the two members is not explicitly concessive because the connecting thought necessary to the full concession is not expressed. We find this phenomenon among the concessions formed with *þeah* (II.11), *hwæðere* (III.1), zero relating element (III.12), concessive-equivalent relative members (IV.11), and other constructions. It seems more than usually common with *ac*, where we have the special disjunctive ellipsis seen in Bo 8/39 and elsewhere, perhaps related to what Wendt calls the *überleitend*, the 'subject-changing' function (III.2).

A further recurrent phenomenon is the parallel member concession, where a single member is in concessive relation with a number of concessive members which are syntactically parallel, often as poetical variations. This is found with *þeah* concessions (II.9), indefinite concessions of degree (IV.6), concessive-equivalent relative members (IV.11), concessive-equivalent clauses of manner (IV.12), of time (IV.13), and of place (IV.14).

A few points concerning the word order and position of concessive members are of special interest. The majority of concessive members follow the members to which they are related, though in a few cases *gyt*-members, for instance, take initial position with the assistance of correlation with the following member (III.7). We have seen that the marked tendency to make dependent *þeah* (*þe*) members follow the related members (II.6) is important for the interpretation of difficult passages, as for instance Beo 1713. Some of the chief patterns of word order in concessive members are as follows: dependent *þeah* (*þe*) members begin with the conjunction and have subject and object or complement preceding the verb (II.5); *ac* is followed by *subject–verb–object, etc.* (III.2), and by *subject–object, etc.–verb*, though sometimes with an important word made disjunctive after *and* (III.3). While *hwæðere* usually introduces its member (III.1), *gyt* normally takes up a medial position (III.7). With zero relating element (III.12), the member in about half the cases begins with a negative particle or a disjunctive word.

There are a few correlative concessive constructions; besides the well-known use of correlation with *þeah* concessions (see II.2), we have for instance *þæs . . . þæt* in indefinite concessions of degree (IV.6), *þa . . . þa, þonne . . . þonne* in concessive-equivalent temporal constructions (IV.13), and *þær . . . þær* in concessive-equivalent local members (IV.14). But considerably more widespread than correlation is reinforcement, the extent of which is perhaps indicated by the reflection that *þeah* is reinforced (by such elements as *swa* and *hwæðere*) in no less than two-thirds of the total nondependent members formed with *þeah* (II.2). Reinforcement of *ac* is unknown in OE verse (III.2), but *and* is quite often reinforced by *gyt, þonne, eft, nu* (III.3), *gyt* by *þa, nu, þonne, (n)æfre* (III.7), concessive-equivalent temporal members once or twice by *ær, efne* (IV.13), concessive-equivalent local members once by *ær* (IV.14), and two-thirds of the concessive equivalent relative members by *ær*[1] (IV.11).

---

1. This feature is also present in the OS version of Gen 802.

We cannot of course say what part intonation played in OE concession, but it is probable that it featured in the 'even' concessive use of *þeah* (II.12) and was used to distinguish the concessive use of *ac* from the adversative (III.2). It seems highly likely that musical means also signaled the concession when there was no relating element (III.12) and gave the concessive-equivalent words and phrases (IV.18f.) their special contextual significance. Stress and intonation no doubt also played a vital role in the concessive use of *wiht* (IV.21).

On the general question of 'even' concession, see 1.2, as well as II.12 where its expression by *þeah* is described. This type of concession is expressed occasionally also with zero relating element (III.12) and is very common with *gyt/gen* (III.7). With zero subordinator and concessive *gif*, the 'even' meaning seems inherent (IV.3, 4), but more frequently it seems to have been expressd with such elements as *furður*, *furðum*, *ne . . . ne*, *ge(. . . ge)*, *eac*, *efne*, *þy* with a comparative, and, the 'even' significance determined by the context of situation, with *an*, *agen*, and *sylf* (IV.20). Commonest of all is *wiht* and prepositional phrases formed with *wiht*; and although it is impossible to tell when this word has its full concessive significance and when it is conventionally emphatic, it seems likely that it has 'even' concessive function in the majority of the poetic examples though rarely in the prose (IV.21).

This indeed is but one of several differences between poetic and prose usage in concessive expression. It would appear from Burnham's monograph, together with an independent survey of a few OE prose texts, that the following are the most important differences. The concessive use of *gyt/gen* is not as frequent in the prose as in the verse, and the prose Bo lacks many of the examples found in the poetic version (III.7). Concessions pointed solely by *hwæðere* are rare in the prose but constitute more than 5 per cent of poetic concessions (III.1). On the other hand, *ac*, which is used in less than 3 per cent of the poetic concessions, is very frequent in prose concessions (III.2); even so, the poetic proportion is made unnaturally high by the 12 examples of *ac* in Bo (more than in any other poetic text) which derive chiefly from the prose original. Nondependent member concessions formed without relating element (III.12) seem rare in the prose but are very frequent in the poetry.

Among the dependent concessive constructions, the alternative concession (IV.2) shows most points of difference between prose and poetic usage. In the first place, alternative concession—indeed concession as a whole—seems much more frequent in the verse than in prose, a contrast epitomized by the relation of Bo to its source. Secondly, while the *swa . . . swa* construction is used in the verse, we do not find *swæðer* used with it as it is in some prose. Thirdly, the individual constructions are either chiefly or entirely confined to one or other medium; the *ge*(... *ge*) form which is rare in the verse is common in prose; the constructions with *oððe* and *ne* which are common in verse seem rare in prose; the prose constructions 'beo he ... beo he,' 'wolde he nolde he,' 'sam ... sam' are absent from the verse.

The position is similar with indefinite concessions of degree, where the *swa plus adjective* construction is confined to prose and the *þæs plus adjective* construction confined to verse (IV.6). In concessive-equivalent clauses of manner, the recurrent 'disapproval' pattern ('swa hit no sceolde') appears to be confined to the poetry (IV.12) and is introduced into Bo and ParPs without warrant from the OE prose and the Latin source respectively. In the concessive-equivalent degree members (IV.17), the poetry never uses the construction *swa ... swa*, which is the normal prose form, but always *þy ... þe*, which is first recorded in prose in ASC E 1140. Finally, the verse seems to use *wiht* concessively to a great extent whereas the prose does so but rarely (IV.21).

The poetic version of Bo is on the whole remarkably faithful to its prose source; sometimes whole sentences appear unaltered apart from slight changes necessary to meet the technical demands of the alliterative measure; two typical features of prose usage, the high proportion of concessions with *ac* and the low proportion of concessions with *hwæðere*, are witnesses to this fidelity. It is therefore interesting confirmation of the distinctions we have observed between prose and poetic usage to find that two of the four instances of *hwæðere* in Bo are replacements of *þeah* concessions, the other two being without corresponding concessions in the prose. As this last point would suggest, Bo is also true to its poetic style in being more liberal with concession as a whole. It introduces the 'disapproving' concessive expression 'swa hit gedefe ne wæs' (Bo 26/92), without warrant from the original, and it breaks up the typical prose forms *nanwuht, nauht* into the typical poetic forms *ne ... wuhte, auht ne*.

In the concessions formed with *þeah*, the distinction between indicative and subjunctive verbs corresponds almost exactly to the distinction between grammatically nondependent and dependent; thus in Bo 29/89 we find the versifier making a dependent *þeah*-member with the subjunctive where his source had a nondependent *þeah*-member with the indicative. There are only a few exceptional cases of dependent *þeah*-members having indicative verbs (II.7). In indefinite concessions of degree, there is one example of the subjunctive (IV.6); the 'challenge' construction, used in indefinite relative concessions ('whoever' IV.7, 'whatever' IV.8), is formed with the subjunctive, and we find this mood also in the indefinite concessions of place, whether of the 'challenge' type or not (IV.9). Finally, concessive-equivalent temporal and local members (IV.13, 14), which usually have the indicative, are recorded also with subjunctive verbs.

Since the texts which Burnham analyzes are predominantly direct translations from the Latin, it is not remarkable that she finds in them " considerable Latin influence upon the concessive expression." Yet, even from this material, she is able to conclude that " the independence of the native idiom is marked" (p. 126). There is little evidence of Latin influence in the poetry. In ParPs there are many more concessions than in the Latin original, and even where the OE concession corresponds to one in the Latin, there is not usually any close correspondence of form, position, or word order. Frequently, it is true, concessions with zero relating element often correspond to the same type of concessive construction in the Latin, and concessions with *and* often translate concessions with *et,* but since these two forms are widespread throughout OE poetry one cannot talk of 'influence' in the correspondence. On the other hand, the "independence of the native idiom" is shown by the fact that zero relating element corresponds also to concessions with *et, etenim, et tamen,* the *cum* construction, and especially to *vero, autem,* and *sed* (III.12); similarly, *and* corresponds not only to *et* but to *rursus, ecce tamen, autem,* and *cum* (III.3). These examples show not only independence in the choice of relating element but also in making nondependent concessions correspond to dependent. On the other hand, *ac*, which as we have seen is not greatly used for concession in OE poetry, usually corresponds more directly to the Latin forms, *sed, autem,* or *verum* (III.2). But although the foregoing examples have shown Latin concessions rendered by similar or less formal OE constructions, the tendency usually is to have the concession more strongly expressed in the OE. Thus while *hwæðere* often corresponds directly to *veruntamen*, it just as frequently translates a less formally expressed concession (III.1), and this applies even more to *þeah* constructions, both dependent and nondependent, which are often used to translate such concessive-equivalent constructions as the participial expression ' cornua producentem,' ParPs 68/31 (II.15). We find a nondependent *nu*-member once translating an *autem*-member and once a *cum*-clause (III.8), and a concessive-equivalent manner clause with *swa* once translates a *veruntamen*-member, exchanging dependent expression for nondependent (IV.12). While concessive-equivalent relative members may correspond to relative members so used in the Latin also, the Latin lacks anything like the reinforcing *ær* of the OE construction (IV.11), and most of the examples of concessively asseverating *wiht* in ParPs have nothing to correspond in the Latin (IV.21).

Even the closest correspondence of construction does not usually extend to correspondence of word order or position. When *hwæðere* translates *verumtamen*, it nevertheless takes initial position in the member (III.1), and when in ParPs 68/5 the Latin concessive-equivalent relative member is put initially, the corresponding OE relative member takes up the normal native final position (IV.11). Similarly, the OE dependent *þeah*-members predominantly take up final position whatever the position of the concessive members they translate (II.6). The only notable example of imitation of Latin word order is in the use of *þonne* with nondependent member concessions in ParPs; eight times we find *þonne* translating *vero* or *autem* and like these preceded in the member by one word only (III.10).

In short, concession in OE could take a much wider variety of forms, was in much more frequent use, was capable of far greater precision and effectiveness, and, even in its most grammatically complex forms, owed much less to the imitation of Latin models than has been supposed.

Selected Bibliography

1. TEXTS

CHAMBERS, R. W., see Wyatt, A. J.
COOK, A. S., *Judith, an Old English Epic Fragment*, Boston, Heath, 1904.
DICKINS, B., ROSS, A. S. C., *The Dream of the Rood*, London, Methuen, 1934.
DOBBIE, E. V. K., *The Anglo-Saxon Minor Poems*, New York, Columbia University Press, 1942 (ASPR VI).
GILES, J. A., *The Complete Works of the Venerable Bede*, London, Whittaker, 1843.
GOLLANCZ, I., *The Exeter Book*, Part I (EETS.OS 104), London, 1895.
GREIN, C. W. M., WÜLKER, R. P., *Bibliothek der angelsächsischen Poesie*, Kassel, G. H. Wigand, 1883–98.
KLAEBER, F., *Beowulf*, 3d ed., Boston, Heath, 1936.
KRÄMER, E., *Die altenglischen Metra des Boethius* (Bonner Breiträge zur Anglistik, 8), Bonn, 1902.
KRAPP, G. P., *The Junius Manuscript*, New York, Columbia University Press, 1931 (ASPR I).
——— *The Vercelli Book*, New York, Columbia University Press, 1932 (ASPR II).
——— *The Paris Psalter and the Meters of Boethius*, New York, Columbia University Press, 1933 (ASPR V).
——— DOBBIE, E. V. K., *The Exeter Book*, New York, Columbia University Press, 1936 (ASPR III).
MACKIE, W. S., *The Exeter Book*, Part II (EETS.OS 194), London, 1933.
MARRIOTT, J. W., *Best One-Act Plays of 1946–1947*, London, Harrap, 1947.
PLUMMER, C., EARLE, J., *Two of the Saxon Chronicles Parallel*, Oxford, Clarendon Press, 1892.
PLUMMER, C., *Venerabilis Baedae Opera Historica*, Oxford, Clarendon Press, 1896.

SEDGEFIELD, W. J., *King Alfred's Old English Version of Boethius De Consolatione Philosophiae*, Oxford, Clarendon Press, 1899.

SMITH, A. H., *Three Northumbrian Poems*, London, Methuen, 1933.

SWEET, H., *King Alfred's Orosius* (EETS.OS 79), London, 1883.

THORPE, B., *Libri Psalmorum*, Oxford, Oxford University Press, 1835.

TIMMER, B. J., *The Later Genesis*, Oxford, Scrivener Press, 1948.

WÜLKER, R. P., see Grein, C. W. M.

WYATT, A. J., *Old English Riddles*, Boston, Heath, 1912.

——— CHAMBERS, R. W., *Beowulf*, 3d ed., Cambridge, Cambridge University Press, 1925.

2. GENERAL

ADAMS, A., *The Syntax of the Temporal Clause in Old English Prose* (Yale Studies in English 32), New York, 1907.

ANDREW, S. O., *Syntax and Style in Old English*, Cambridge, Cambridge University Press, 1940.

——— *Postscript on Beowulf*, Cambridge, Cambridge University Press, 1948.

BEHAGHEL, O., *Deutsche Syntax: ein geschichtliche Darstellung*, Bd. III: *Die Satzgebilde*, Heidelberg, Germanische Bibliothek, 1928.

BEHRE, F., *The Subjunctive in Old English Poetry* (Göteborgs Högskolas Årsskrift 40), Gothenburg, 1934.

BLOOMFIELD, L., 'Old English Plural Subjunctives in *e*,' JEGPh xxix. 100–13.

——— *Language*, London, G. Allen & Unwin, 1935.

BØGHOLM, N., *The Layamon Texts, a Linguistical Investigation*, Copenhagen, Arnold Busck, 1944.

BOSKER, A., 'Some Aspects of the Study of English Syntax,' Neophil xxxi.28–43.

BOSWORTH, J., *An Anglo-Saxon Dictionary*, ed. T. N. Toller, Oxford, Clarendon Press, 1898.

——— *An Anglo-Saxon Dictionary*, Supplemented by T. N. Toller, Oxford, Clarendon Press, 1921.

BRODEUR, A. G., 'The Climax of the Finn Episode,' *Univ. of California Publications in English* iii No. 8.

BRUNNER, K., *Altenglische Grammatik, nach der angelsächsischen Grammatik von Eduard Sievers*, Halle, Niemeyer, 1942.

BRUNOT, F., *La Pensée et la langue*, 3d ed., Paris, Masson, 1936.
BURNHAM, J. M., *Concessive Constructions in Old English Prose* (Yale Studies in English 39), New York, 1911.
CALLAWAY, M., *The Absolute Participle in Anglo-Saxon*, Baltimore, I. Friedenwald, 1889.
───── 'The Appositive Participle in Anglo-Saxon,' PMLA xvi. 141–360.
───── *Studies in the Syntax of the Lindisfarne Gospels* (Hesperia: Supp. Series 5), Baltimore, 1918.
CHARLESTON, B. M., *Studies on the Syntax of the English Verb* (Schweizer Anglistische Arbeiten 11), Bern, 1941.
CHASE, F. H., 'The Absolute Participle in the Old English Apollonius,' MLN viii.486–9.
COBB, G. W., 'The Subjunctive Mood in Old English Poetry,' *Philologica*, ed. T. A. Kirby and H. B. Woolf, Baltimore, Johns Hopkins Press, 1949, pp. 43–55.
COLLINSON, W. E., 'Some Recent Trends in Linguistic Theory, with Special Reference to Syntactics,' Lingua i.306–32.
───── 'Some Recent Developments of Syntactical Theory,' Phil Soc 1941, pp. 43–133.
CURME, G. O., *Syntax*, Boston, Heath, 1931.
DELBRÜCK, B., 'Der germanische Optativ im Satzgefüge,' PBBeit xxix.201–304.
DUBISLAV, G., 'Studien zu me. Syntax,' Anglia xl.263, 297; xlv.51, 283; xlvi.239.
EINENKEL, E., *Geschichte der englischen Sprache*, II: *Historische Syntax*, 3d ed., Strassburg, K. J. Trübner, 1916.
ERICSON, E. E., 'The Use of Old English swa in Negative Clauses,' *Studies in Honor of Hermann Collitz*, Baltimore, Johns Hopkins Press, 1930, pp. 159–75.
───── *The Use of swa in Old English*, Baltimore, Johns Hopkins Press, 1932.
FIELD, H. F., 'Comparative Syntax and Some Modern Theories of the Subjunctive,' MPh xxiii.201–24.
FOURQUET, J., *L'Ordre des éléments de la phrase en Germanique Ancien*, Paris, Publications de la Faculté des Lettres de l'Université de Strasbourg, 1938.
GLUNZ, H., *Die Verwendung des Konjunktivs im Altenglischen*, Leipzig, B. Tauchnitz, 1929.
GREIN, C. W. M., HOLTHAUSEN, F., KÖHLER, J. J., *Sprachschatz der angelsächsischen Dichter*, Heidelberg, C. Winter, 1912.

HALE, W. G., 'The *Cum*-Constructions: Their History and Functions,' StClPhil i.1–264.

HALL, J. R. C., *A Concise Anglo-Saxon Dictionary*, 3d ed., Cambridge, Cambridge University Press, 1931.

HEUSLER, A., *Altisländisches Elementarbuch*, Heidelberg, C. Winter, 1921.

HIRT, H. A., *Handbuch des Urgermanischen*, Heidelberg, C. Winter, 1931–34.

HOLTHAUSEN, F., *Altsächsisches Elementarbuch*, Heidelberg, C. Winter, 1921.

HORN, W., 'Untersuchungen zur historischen englischen Syntax,' Archiv cliv.213–23.

JESPERSEN, O., *A Modern English Grammar*, Parts II-IV, Heidelberg, C. Winter, 1914–27; Parts V-VII, London, G. Allen & Unwin, 1946–49.

——— 'A System of Clauses,' SPE liv.157–71.

JOHNSEN, O., 'On Some Uses of the Indefinite Relatives in Old English,' Anglia xxxvii.281–302, 392.

KELLNER, L., *Historical Outlines of English Syntax*, London, Macmillan, 1892.

KENNEDY, C. W., *The Poems of Cynewulf*, New York, E. P. Dutton, 1910.

KRUISINGA, E., 'How to Study Old English Syntax' EngSts viii.44–9.

——— *A Handbook of Present-Day English*, Utrecht, Kemink, 1925.

KUHLMANN, H., *Die Konzessivsätze im Nibelungenliede und in der Kudrun*, Leipzig, G. Fock, 1891.

LERCH, E., *Historische französische Syntax*, Leipzig, O. R. Reisland, 1925–34.

MAISENHELDER, K., *Die altenglische Partikel " and,"* Königsfeld, H. Stolz, 1935.

MANN, G., *Konjunktionen und Modus im konsekutiven und finalen Nebensatz des Altenglischen*, Breslau, Priebatsch, 1939.

MATHER, F. J., *The Conditional Sentence in Anglo-Saxon*, Munich, C. Wolf, 1893.

MÄTZNER, E., *Englische Grammatik*, Berlin, Weidmann, 1880–85.

MENSING, O., *Untersuchungen über die Syntax der Concessivsätze im Alt- und Mittelhochdeutschen*, Leipzig, G. Fock, 1891.

MERONEY, H., 'Old English ðær " if," ' JEGPh xli.201–9.

MORRIS, E. P., *On Principles and Methods in Latin Syntax*, New York, Scribner, 1901.

MOSSÉ, F., *Manuel de l'Anglais du Moyen Âge*, I: *Vieil-Anglais*, Paris, Aubier, 1945; II: *Moyen-Anglais*, Paris, Aubier, 1949.

MURRAY, J., BRADLEY, H., CRAIGIE, W. A., ONIONS, C. T., *A New English Dictionary on Historical Principles*, Oxford, Clarendon Press, 1888–1933.

OHLANDER, U., *Studies on Coordinate Expressions in Middle English*, Lund, Gleerup, 1936.

ONIONS, C. T., *An Advanced English Syntax*, 6th ed., London, Paul, Trench, Trubner & Co., 1932.

POUTSMA, H., *A Grammar of Late Modern English*, Groningen, Noordhoff, 1926–29.

RÜBENS, G., *Parataxe und Hypotaxe in dem älteren Teil der Sachsenchronik*, StudEngPhil lvi.

RUSSELL, B., *An Inquiry into Meaning and Truth*, London, G. Allen & Unwin, 1940.

SANDMANN, M., ' Subordination and Coordination ' ArchLing ii.24–38.

―――― ' On Linguistic Explanation,' MLR xxxvi.195–212.

SARRAZIN, G., *Von Kädmon bis Kynewulf*, Berlin, Mayer & Müller, 1913.

SCHUBIGER, M., *The Role of Intonation in Spoken English*, Cambridge, W. Heffer, 1935.

―――― ' English Intonation and Syntax,' *Proceedings of the Second International Congress of Phonetic Sciences*, Cambridge, Cambridge University Press, 1935, 87–92.

SCHÜCKING, L. L., *Die Grundzüge der Satzverknüpfung im Beowulf*, StudEngPhil xv.

SHEARIN, H. G., Review of J. M. Burnham, *Concessive Constructions in Old English Prose*, MLN xxvi.255–8.

SMALL, G. W., ' On the Study of Old English Syntax,' PMLA li.1–7.

―――― Review of U. Ohlander, *Studies on Coordinate Expressions in Middle English*, JEGPh xxxvii.291–5.

SONNENSCHEIN, E. A., *A New English Grammar*, Part III, Oxford, Clarendon Press, 1924.

―――― *The Soul of Grammar*, Cambridge, Cambridge University Press, 1927.

STEBBING, L. S., *A Modern Introduction to Logic*, 2d ed., London, Methuen, 1933.

STOFFEL, C., *Intensives and Downtoners*, Heidelberg, C. Winter, 1901.

STREITBERG, W., *Gotisches Elementarbuch*, 2d ed., Heidelberg, C. Winter, 1906.

SWEET, H., *A New English Grammar*, Oxford, Clarendon Press, 1892–98.

TOLLER, T. N., see Bosworth, J.

TRNKA, B., *Syntaktická Charakteristika Řeči Anglosaských památek básnických* ('A Syntactical Analysis of the Language of Anglo-Saxon Poetry'), Studies in English (Prague University), Prague, 1925.

WENDT, G., *Syntax des heutigen Englisch*, Heidelberg, C. Winter, 1911–14.

WESTERN, A., *De Engelske Bisætninger: en Historisk-Syntaktisk Studie*, Kristiania, J. W. Cappelen, 1893.

WILDE, H.-O., 'Aufforderung, Wunsch und Möglichkeit,' Anglia lxiii. 209–391; lxiv.10–105.

WILLIAMS, R. A., *The Finn Episode in Beowulf*, Cambridge, Cambridge University Press, 1924.

WILMANNS, W., *Deutsche Grammatik*, Part III, Strassburg, K. J. Trübner, 1906.

WÜLFING, J. E., *Die Syntax in den Werken Alfreds des Grossen*, Bonn, P. Hanstein, 1894–1901.

Index

This index lists poetic references of special interest, as well as subjects and forms not readily found from the chapter and section headings.

adversative relation: 4, 51f, 75
ær: 105ff, 113
agen: 124
an: 124
And 629: 58
And 811: 15, 21

Beo 166: 74
Beo 599: 53f
Beo 967: 95
Beo 1129: 36
Beo 1612–3: 31, 33
Beo 1713: 17, 28
Beo 2124: 80
Beo 2466–7: 31, 33, 40
Beo 2570: 109
Beo 2724: 122
Bo 19/1, 20/26: 99
Bo 29/49–52: 31, 33

'chain' concession: 75f
Charm 4/18–24: 89f
Chr 367: 28
Chr 1418–9: 30, 33
Chr 1424: 61f
ChrSat 405: 57f
correlation: 14ff, 61, 66, 86, 106, 113

disjunction: 23f, 77f

eac: 124f
efne: 37, 71, 113, 118, 125f
eft: 71
elliptical concession: 9, 36f, 45f, 49f, 75, 104
Ex 61: 122
Ex 538: 111
Exhort 16: 100

for-: 96
formulaic structure: 66f, 76f, 78, 110ff
furðum, furður: 65, 69, 124f

ge: 37, 84, 86, 124
Gen 391: 108, 110f
Gen 531: 39
Gen 661: 7, 89
Gen 733–6: 30, 33

Gen 830: 95, 97
Gen 1564: 111
Gen 1953: 128
Gl 226: 53
Gl 271: 104f
Gl 479, 1064: 28

Hell 64: 97
huru: 17, 70, 125
Husband 35–9: 31f
hwæt: 70

imperative, use of: 80f, 100
inversion constructions: 84, 87f, 94f

Jud I 12: 109f
Jul 87: 100
Jul 216: 28
Jul 490–2: 30ff

Menol 63: 52f

(n)æfre: 66, 95
negative expressions: 18f, 34, 53f, 77, 79f, 85ff, 95f, 110f, 124, 129ff
no þy ær: 11, 18, 72, 79f
nu: 18, 66ff, 112f, 115f

oððe: 84f, 87
ofer: 121f
Order 23: 96

ParPs 62/8: 60
participial expressions: 122f
Pharaoh 4: 62f

reference, conventions for: 3f
reinforcement: 14ff, 48, 56, 65f, 69, 110, 113
Rid 48/1: 23
Rid 72/17: 89
Rid 95/10: 31, 33

sam: 84, 87
Seaf 55 (33, 39, 64): 58ff
Sol 364: 87
Soul I 62: 123
Soul I 135: 16, 18, 22, 30, 32

Soul I 144: 88
subjunctive, distinctive forms of: 10, 12, 29
swa: 13, 15, 17, 19ff, 39, 41, 84, 86, 93, 96f, 100f, 108ff, 117f, 121
swylce: 71
sylf: 124
symle: 71

temporal elements: 17f, 63ff, 105ff, 112ff
terminology: 4ff, 14f, 50, 52

þa: 18, 66, 68f, 112ff
þær: 71, 101, 114f
þæs: 72, 95ff, 115f
þæt: 96f, 100, 116
þe, þeah accompanied by: 21ff, 35, 39f, 41
þonan: 71
þonne: 18, 44, 66, 69f, 92, 112ff
þy with comparative (see also *no þy ær*): 18f, 79f, 117f

Wife 15, 37: 59f